Gun Dog BREEDS

Books by Charles Fergus

The Wingless Crow
Shadow Catcher (a novel)
A Rough-Shooting Dog
Wildlife of Pennsylvania and the Northeast
Natural Pennsylvania: Exploring the State Forest Natural Areas
Summer at Little Lava: A Season at the Edge of the World
Rabbit Hunting
Gun Dog Breeds

Gun Dog
BREEDS

A Guide to
Spaniels,
Retrievers,
and
Pointing Dogs

CHARLES FERGUS

Foreword by
A. Hamilton Rowan, Jr.

THE LYONS PRESS
Guilford, CT 06437
An imprint of The Globe Pequot Press

The Lyons Press is an imprint of The Globe Pequot Press

Manufactured in the United States of America

10 9 8 7 6 5 4 3 2 1

ISBN: 1-58574-618-5

Library of Congress Cataloging-in-Publication data is available on file.

All photographs are by the author except the following:

  A. Hamilton Rowan, Jr.: Boykin spaniel, golden retriever, wirehaired pointing
     griffon
  Vivien Surmen: Sussex spaniel

For BOB BELL

Contents

Acknowledgments

I thank the following people for their help in making this book: Dianne Russell, who suggested the topic; Hamilton Rowan, Nick Headings, John Schaeffer, Roberta Vesley, Ruth Fergus, Nancy Marie Brown, Richard Fortmann, Anne Crowley, Sandy Roth, Bonnie Jacobs, and the many others who generously loaned me books, gave me information on their favorite breeds, and let me photograph their dogs.

I also thank Jon and Lou Scheckler of Scheckler Photographics, State College, Pennsylvania, for their excellent advice concerning photography and their fine printing of many of the black-and-white images in this book.

Foreword

W hen Charles Fergus asked me to write the Foreword to his new guide to the gun dog breeds, I was quite hesitant. After all, what *more* or *new* could possibly be written about these dogs? But I knew Fergus both personally and through his several previously published works. I accepted because I felt sure he would find something new that needed to be told. He has, in fact, written a delightfully readable, important book, a most useful and trustworthy guide to the spaniels, retrievers, and pointing-breed dogs that work effectively as canine hunting companions.

The fact that you have sought out this book would be an indication that you have an interest in the gun dog breeds. Breed choice, as Fergus points out, is a very personal decision. It involves decisions on such matters as size, color, long coat/short coat, game to be hunted, and, is "Thud" to be a house or a kennel dog?

How I wish that this book had been available to me some fifty years ago! Even though I had learned to hunt over trained gun dogs as a youth in my native England, it was obvious after settling in the United States after World War II, and then wanting a gun dog, that my knowledge of these breeds did not apply to their American counterparts.

My first dog was a cocker spaniel who developed an insatiable fetish for sinking her teeth into human legs. My next dog was a beagle from a New Hampshire farm, who spent most nights in full cry after rabbits in our Long Island suburb. Not until I developed a friendship with a local breeder of German shorthaired pointers did I acquire the first of a continuing line of wonderful canine hunting companions.

In the last thirty years, innumerable books and magazine articles have been published whose purpose is simply to help the reader gain general knowledge about the approximately three hundred dog breeds that exist worldwide. Of these, 132 are eligible for registration in the stud book of the American Kennel Club. There is a monotonous sameness about these writings, because most of the material has been extracted and recycled from previously published works. Only the pictures are different.

Much of this source material comes from the AKC's *Complete Dog Book*, which professes to acquaint the public with the appearance and qualifications of each breed. Its 132 breed histories, each authored by an unidentified expert, are self-serving, ingenuous, and more often misleading—particularly in respect to the temperament and working capabilities of the breeds.

Because Fergus does not have to answer to any higher authorities, he is able to provide the reader with a completely unbiased and accurate assessment of the hunting effectiveness and temperament for each breed. He is also sufficiently frank to raise a storm warning about serious genetic health problems that are known to occur in specimens of some of the gun dog breeds—a sensitive matter that many dog writers avoid.

The dictates of regional domicile play a large part in breed choice, so that most people looking for a gun dog already know what game they want to hunt, or what local game is available. Fergus candidly points out the game species that can be pursued effectively using each of the gun dog breeds—to my knowledge, a first.

In Fergus's ever-consummate literary style, and from his excellent research and solid hunting experience, he has succeeded in designing this book to, in his words, "help the hunter, beginner or veteran, find the breed best suited to his or her choice of game, style of hunting, temperament, training facilities, and situation in life." His assessments of the hunt-worthiness of each breed are uncommonly frank. He cautions repeatedly that if you are really serious about owning a good hunter, you must be absolutely certain that your dog comes from proven hunting stock. The pitfalls in this regard are very real; and always remember that "Thud" will be your hunting partner for at least the next ten years. The decisions you must make are similar to those of child adoption.

The author's honesty and candid breed assessments will only startle the "kennel blind" and those readers with preconceived notions about the hunting effectiveness of a certain breed. I admonish them with the old adage that sometimes the truth hurts. Most dogs are nice to their masters. Fergus, however, is looking for more than "niceness" in a breed in order for him to qualify it as a consistent source of effective, healthy, canine hunting companions.

Fergus understands and appreciates the meaning of the words "hunting companion dog." He has experienced all of the emotions of having such a dog become a member of his household and his hunting companion—all so eloquently told in his recent book, *A Rough-Shooting Dog.*

Like Fergus, the companionship of a dog of one of the hunting breeds is still a necessity when I am afield, for whatever reason.

On a hunting trip, my dog is the perfect traveling companion. And, of course, she locates and then retrieves all shot game.

As I write this piece in my study, I am being watched by four incredibly talented and much-loved gun dogs. One of them, Dixie, a nine-year-old Boykin spaniel, is asleep on the couch, with one eye half open to catch any motion I might make toward the dog whistles hanging alongside the window. The other three, two German shorthaired pointers and a Brittany spaniel, gaze down at me from their painted portraits. They have been my closest hunting companions during the past fifty years, and all have been members of our household. Each one has given me exciting memories of times spent together in the fields, woods, marshes, and alder tags.

It's early October once again. The woodcock season opened two days ago. This evening, Dixie and I re-enacted a situation so eloquently described by my friend and fellow countryman, Ken Roebuck, the distinguished author and gun dog trainer:

> Crisp flushed the final woodcock of the day. We
> watched it flicker through the trees in silhouette, and
> wished it well.

It's almost impossible to experience such wondrous moments without a dog—and even more difficult to explain them on paper. They must be lived. Charles Fergus would understand. Get a gun dog and you will, too.

A. Hamilton Rowan, Jr.
Former Director of
Field Trials and Hunting Tests,
American Kennel Club
October 1991

Men are generally more careful of the breed of their horses and dogs than of their children.

—WILLIAM PENN
Reflexions and Maxims

Introduction

*Moon is beside me, tired now
too, throwing his own pale
dog-shadow ahead. And the
hunter-shadow with him, the
pheasant hanging from the
hunter's belt, snipe bulging in
the jacket.*

—VANCE BOURJAILY
In Fields Near Home

Without a dog you can still hunt birds. You can learn the haunts
and habits of wildfowl, beat the coverts, slip through the
marshes, and bring back a harvest of solace, self-understanding,
and game.

Yet to hunt with a dog—to league yourself with an animal bred
and honed for the hunt, whose form, character, and identity are
determined and defined by its purpose—is to become more completely involved in this basic natural endeavor. I had heard hunters say they would not hunt if they could not do so in company
with a dog; I only half believed them. Then I myself got one, and

took a quantum jump in my effectiveness as a hunter and in my enjoyment and understanding of the hunt. If life's circumstances changed and I found myself dogless, I might go on hunting, but it would be a secondhand sort of thing.

A dog will amplify your senses. It will sniff out game you alone would never have found. It will signal the presence of birds in advance, and it will run down and recover wounded ones. Its enthusiasm will infect you. It will bring friendship and love to the joint venture of the hunt. Its very presence will keep you focused on the task at hand: You will perceive the world—and your place in it—in a new and expanded way.

When I think back on hunts I have made, the best have been with dogs. The pointer crouched on the fringe of a cloud of woodcock scent, the bird invisible in the mosaic of fallen leaves until I took one more step and flushed it. The spaniel, yanked around sideways by bird scent, redirecting its charge, the suddenly besieged pheasant blooming from the grass. The retriever, whose upraised eyes bulged wider, the dog's ears pricking and its tail brooming the creekbank mud: Soon the falling-leaf shapes of ducks would reflect in those amber orbs.

I did not need to kill a bird to remember those days or those dogs. It was enough simply to share their fire.

Humans have let dogs help them hunt since time out of mind. Who knows how the partnership evolved? Perhaps bands of hunters were followed by packs of wild dogs. The canines scavenged at the humans' kills. Their presence in some way helped the people: Their nighttime barking sounded the alert for prowling lions or bears; their excited cries exposed game; they tracked down wounded prey, the hunters following to dispatch the quarry, then leaving the dogs a portion of the kill.

As centuries passed—and not so very many of them—dogs earned places in the homes of humans. Worldwide, agriculture arose and became dominant, the human population burgeoned, and hunting changed from a necessity to an occasional pastime, a humbling of self to the status of animal in the hierarchy of animals, a personal ceremony hearkening back to our roots. And the dog stayed on, hunting with us.

The veneer of breeding is a thin one: Let purebred dogs mate outside of their lineage, and in two or three generations all that will be left is a mongrel bearing no resemblance to its forebears. How plastic, this creature *Canis familiaris:* Breeds arise, thrive, are used as foundation stock for other breeds, change size or coat length or conformation or color, fall out of fashion, disappear. (How fickle, this creature *Homo sapiens.*)

Some of the hunting breeds are centuries old. One of the breeds covered in this book arose wholly during the twentieth century. All are fascinating; all have histories; all have human adherents (some of them fanatical); and all are beautiful in their own way, exemplified by the individual animal who knows its task and performs it capably and spiritedly in the field.

Gun Dog Breeds describes the dogs used to hunt North American wildfowl: upland birds (pheasants, grouse, woodcock, quail); plains species (sage grouse, prairie chickens, Hungarian partridge); doves; shorebirds (snipe and rails); and waterfowl (ducks and geese). There is no bias toward any category or breed. This book is designed to help the hunter, beginner or veteran, find the breed best suited to his or her choice of game, style of hunting, temperament, training facilities, and situation in life. It covers breeds both popular and obscure. It does not explain how to train dogs; there are many fine works on that subject.

The book is divided into three main sections.

Flushing Spaniels find, flush, and fetch game—as they have done for more than a thousand years. They work primarily on land but also retrieve from the water.

Retrievers fetch back killed or wounded game from land or water. Most can be taught to hunt before the gun like flushing spaniels.

Pointing Dogs have a specialized, highly refined function: They signal game by stopping and standing motionless until the hunter approaches. Pointing dogs may also be capable retrievers.

The final two chapters give advice on how to choose a breed, locate a litter, and pick a puppy. An Appendix lists pertinent organizations. Where given, addresses of breed clubs are current for 1991. If, after writing to a club, you receive no answer, check with the American Kennel Club or Field Dog Stud Book for an up-to-date address.

Finally, a note concerning style: If a breed name includes a proper noun, only that word is capitalized; for instance, Welsh springer spaniel, Gordon setter, Chesapeake Bay retriever—as opposed to field spaniel, pointer, golden retriever.

I

FLUSHING SPANIELS

*Crisp flushed the final wood-
cock of the day. We watched it
flicker through the trees in
silhouette, and wished it well.*

—KENNETH ROEBUCK
Bronx House Woodcock

Legend has it that Roman legionnaires brought the first spaniels to the British Isles when they invaded in A.D. 43. There the dog flourished. By the late Middle Ages the type had split into two lines: water spaniels, used to hunt waterfowl (these dogs would develop into today's retrievers); and land spaniels: "Another kind of hound there is that be called hounds for the hawk and spaniels, for their kind cometh from Spain, notwithstanding that there are many in other countries." So wrote Edward, second Duke of York, in *The Master of Game*, the oldest work on hunting in the English language, written around 1406. (Edward was translating from the *Livre de Chasse*, an earlier work by a French nobleman named Gaston de Foix, said to have kept a kennel of a thousand dogs.) "The good qualities that such hounds have are these: they love well their masters and follow them without losing, although they be in a great crowd of men, and commonly they go before their master, running and wagging their tail, and raise or start fowl and wild beasts."

Today's spaniels are not greatly different from their antecedents. Most are loving, vivacious dogs. They have an excellent sense of smell. They beat the cover to roust game from the thickest and thorniest places. Excellent swimmers, they readily cross streams and marshes. They retrieve from both land and water, and are renowned for their "tender" mouths that grip but do not damage the game. Since they flush instead of point their birds, spaniels must work close to the gun. Most are quite trainable, and it takes less effort to restrict their range than it does to steady the more independent pointing breeds.

The fully trained spaniel will quarter the field in a zigzag pattern, keeping an eye on the hunter and staying within twenty yards—closer where the cover is dense. It will flush any bird it scents; then "hup" (sit) until released to hunt onward or fetch. The less than fully trained spaniel will probe likely cover in front of the gunner, stop on command when it reaches the limits of shooting range, flush briskly, and chase after the bird to retrieve it—an adequate performance for most hunters.

Spaniels are great generalists. They fetch doves. They scour the alders for ruffed grouse and woodcock. They root quail out of late-season briars. They work weed fields and cattail bottoms for pheasants. They sit by the hunter's side awaiting the flight of waterfowl. They slog through marshes to jump ducks. Although not built for swimming in heavy seas or making repeated retrieves in frigid weather, they are quite adequate for the upland hunter who spends a few days on the wetlands and creeks each fall. Spaniels are used from California to Maine and from Oregon to Florida on every sort of wildfowl that can be hunted; in England they are even used on rabbits.

There exists a longstanding debate among hunters over flushing spaniels versus pointing dogs. The controversy boils down to two questions: Which sort of dog is more effective? And: Is it aesthetically more pleasing to have the dog flush the bird or point it for the hunter to flush?

In general, birds that gather in coveys, such as bobwhite quail, hold better for pointing dogs than do birds ordinarily encountered as single individuals, like ruffed grouse and pheasant. (Woodcock are an exception: Although most often found singly, they tend to sit tight when pointed.) Early in the season, coveys of ruffed grouse will often hold, but as the birds mature, as they are pursued and shot at, they become wilder and harder for pointing dogs to handle: They simply keep running after the dog has fixed on point, often flushing out of range as well. The ring-necked pheasant is notorious for sneaking off and giving pointing dogs fits; many of the desert quail and prairie grouse species also run.

On running birds, a hunter with a well-controlled flushing spaniel will probably see more shootable game. On the other hand, a pointing dog may help the hunter kill a higher percentage of the birds actually shot at, since the hunter will have more time to get set for each shot.

Use a pointing dog if you concentrate on covey-type birds, a spaniel if you hunt the "single bird" species in dense cover. Some other factors: Wide-ranging pointers quickly disappear in thick, brushy cover, so that when they go on point they are hard to find. Spaniels tend to be better retrievers than most pointing dogs. And spaniels are easier and cheaper to train: Much of the preliminary work can be done in the yard with dummies, rather than in the field with live birds.

Aesthetics? This quotation, from *Shotgunning in the Uplands*, by Ray P. Holland, states an opinion often advanced in the sporting literature: "There is far more thrill in watching a pointing dog than there is in hunting over any of the breeds that flush their game before the gun." Yet the sudden unbridled charge of a spaniel, followed by the vaulting into the air of a brilliant gamebird, is a beautiful and exhilarating thing to see. The fairest conclusion to draw about the aesthetics of the two contrasting styles of dog work is the simplest and most obvious one: To each his own.

Because spaniels are merry and affectionate, they have been bred extensively for pets. Most dogs from pet stock will not make good hunters. Set the odds in your favor by choosing a spaniel out of a proven working line. Eight breeds of spaniel can be had in the United States today: English springer spaniel, Welsh springer spaniel, cocker spaniel, Boykin spaniel, American water spaniel, Clumber spaniel, Sussex spaniel, and field spaniel.

The English springer is *the* working spaniel, a versatile medium-size hunter, by far the most popular sporting spaniel and the standard against which the others must be compared. The Welsh springer is a bit smaller than the English, slower afield and perhaps more thorough in its coverage, a rare breed with much less hunting potential than its English cousin. The cocker spaniel is the old "cocking spaniel"—the smallish spaniel reserved to hunt 'cock, or woodcock (in this book American and English cockers are treated in the same chapter). The American water spaniel is a close-working flusher and fetcher of ducks, grouse, woodcock, and pheasants, used mainly in the upper Midwest. The Boykin spaniel, developed in the South to hunt doves, ducks, and wild turkeys, is a fine all-around performer. Clumber, field, and Sussex spaniels are heavier and slower than the other breeds; relatively rare today, they survive mainly as pets and show dogs, although some retain hunting instincts.

The serious hunter will be best served by an English springer, English cocker (from strictly hunting stock), American water, or Boykin.

In spaniel breeds except the Boykin, dogs and litters are registered with the American Kennel Club. (By contrast, in most pointing breeds, AKC-registered dogs are show stock, and hunting lines within the breeds are registered with the *Field Dog Stud Book.*)

Resources

Gun Dog Training: Spaniels and Retrievers, Kenneth C. Roebuck. Stackpole, Harrisburg, PA, 1982.

Training Spaniels, Joe Irving. David & Charles, North Pomfret, VT, 1980.

The New Complete English Springer Spaniel (contains training information suitable for all spaniels), Charles S. Goodall and Julia Gasow. Howell Book House, New York, 1984.

"Flush" column, Kenneth Roebuck. *Gun Dog* (bimonthly), Stover Publishing, P.O. Box 35098, Des Moines, IA 50315.

Spaniels in the Field (quarterly), Art Rodger, ed., 10714 Escondido Dr., Cincinnati, OH 45249.

The English springer spaniel is a superb all-purpose hunting dog widely available in field bloodlines.

English Springer SPANIEL

Autumn, 1680. With a flick of his hand, a young Englishman sent a brown-and-white spaniel charging into a thicket. The bitch —lean, muscular, with a deep chest that grazed the ground as she ran—pleased the man's eye, as her manner warmed his spirit. A good one, the best from his father's kennel, splendid nose, avid yet tractable—unlike those other half-wild curs, this one would look you in the eye as if trying to divine what it was you wanted. Just the type, he knew, to train for this new way of hunting.

He hefted the flintlock. He had bought the shotgun in France for a pretty penny. His father thought the whole business a farce. Shoot birds flying? 'Tis why we have hawks, son.

The young man slipped into the thicket. The spaniel checked back, a quick glance to see if he was coming, then resumed her quartering, staying nicely within range. She sank her nose in some bracken, her tail whipping. She sprang, and the partridges came up in covey, a gray flaring of six. The young man shouldered the gun, thumbing back the hammer. When he squeezed the trigger, sparks flashed as the flint hit home, and, remembering what his cousin in Normandy had told him, he kept tracking just one bird, swinging the heavy barrel along with the fleeing form— *whump!*, the powder ignited and the gun cuffed his shoulder. Through swirling smoke he saw a partridge fall (not the one he'd aimed at, but no need to tell Father *that*), and the spaniel racing for the downed bird. She took it up in her mouth, turned, and— bless her!—fetched it back. Taking the bird, he grinned at nobody in particular—indeed, no one was along, he hadn't been at all sure how this experiment would turn out. *Shooting flying*, he thought. Even Father would warm to it, he bet.

The flintlock shotgun, invented in the seventeenth century, revolutionized the sport of bird hunting. It made flying shooting (today we call it wingshooting) possible and dog training necessary, and it led to the springer spaniel as we now know it: Hunters had to rein in their spaniels, transform them from riotous beaters into smooth, polished helpers that would hunt within gun range and retrieve the game shot.

The English springer probably developed out of a host of British land spaniels used originally to flush, or "spring," game for hawks and hounds. At one time it was not unusual to have two sorts of spaniels produced in the same litter. Small ones (under twenty-five pounds) were "cocker" spaniels, reserved for woodcock, while the larger "springers" flushed game such as partridges, pheasants, and hares.

Springers became extremely popular throughout Britain. Today they are used widely on "rough shoots," in which gunners take an assortment of game—whatever is rousted out by the dog. Essentially the same sort of hunting is enjoyed in America, and the English springer has caught on here, too, becoming the most popular spaniel breed. Freeman Lloyd, Kennel Editor for *Field and Stream* in the 1930s, labeled the English springer "a dog of all work; the hunter's friend; and the shooting man's complete aid."

The modern English springer stands eighteen to twenty inches at the shoulder and weighs between thirty and fifty pounds, with females slightly smaller and lighter than males. The medium-length coat is flat and wavy (not curly). Although the coat attracts some burs and sticktights, these are generally easily removed. Most English springers are white-and-liver (liver is a dark shade of brown), a few white-and-black. The tail is docked back slightly to about two-thirds of the total length, usually with a white flag left at the tip.

Springers are superb pheasant dogs, unceremoniously hustling ringnecks into the air. They do excellent work on ruffed grouse and woodcock in heavy cover. They sit quietly until sent to fetch doves and ducks. Strong swimmers, they retrieve naturally from the water. They probe the marsh in front of hip-booted hunters, putting ducks to flight and then fetching them, tracking down cripples over long distances. In the West they are used on spooky late-season sharp-tailed grouse. In the South they root quail out of thick briars in winter. They start up snipe and rail from the wet bottoms. . . . In short, a good springer will hunt any sort of fowl in any type of cover.

Which is not to say they are the best breed for all game and all hunting situations. The retrievers outdo them at fetching waterfowl, especially in frigid weather. The pointing dogs cover more ground, and do a better job on covey birds such as quail in open country or in patches of cover separated by long distances. But for the hunter who pursues a gamut of gamebirds, and who does not demand that the birds be pointed, the English springer will do a creditable job on any species encountered.

The English springer has an excellent nose—better, most experts agree, than its chief multipurpose competitor, the Labrador retriever. The springer hunts in front of the gun, questing for body or foot scent. When it detects foot scent, it puts its nose down and puzzles out the trail, alerting the hunter with its thrashing tail. Zeroing in on the quarry and picking up body scent, it lifts its head for the final lunge—and the harried gamebird takes to the air before it is caught.

A well-trained springer covers the ground in a looping zigzag pattern, pushing out and ahead on each side and drifting back in toward the hunter as it crosses in front. If a running bird draws the spaniel ahead, one blast on the whistle hups the dog—makes it sit—before the chase gets beyond gun range. The hunter moves into position, then releases the spaniel. After flushing the bird, the dog again hups: This lets it clearly mark the bird for a re- trieve, keeps it out of the shot pattern, and prevents it from bumping another bird while chasing the first. After the shot, the dog is sent to fetch or, if the bird was missed, released to hunt onward.

Steadying an English springer to flush and shot takes extensive training. Fortunately, one can fall short of this ideal and still have an excellent hunting companion. The average springer will quick- ly learn to quarter, explore the cover, work the thick, thorny places where game is often found. It will respond to whistle and hand signals, checking out patches of cover on command. With a not-unreasonable amount of effort, it can be trained to hup on whistle, to prevent it from flushing birds out of range and to leave off chasing missed birds.

Springers have engaging personalities and an appealingly ea- ger style afield. Biddable and anxious to please, they learn quick- ly and retain what they're taught. If started properly, they mature earlier than many other breeds and can be hunting proficiently by the time they're one year old. Some individuals are "soft," requiring leniency and care during training, but most will readily accept discipline fairly meted out. Too, springers can be stubborn, ingratiatingly working to get their own way; as with all breeds, they require a consistent, vigilant trainer. In general, it is easier to bring an English springer up to a reasonable level of effectiveness than it is to train one of the pointing breeds to an equivalent level.

Although rugged enough to be kenneled outside, springers make excellent house pets. Their size suits them to apartments and small houses. Good watchdogs, they will bark at strangers or suspicious noises. Field-bred springers are quite subordinate to humans—even young children who pull their ears and flail them over the head.

The difference between show and field English springers is immense. Show springers (or pets out of show lines) are larger and heavier-boned than are their field-bred counterparts; they have longer fur, longer and more pendent ears, dewlaps and dangling flews, and a docked stub tail—the dog typically shown on dog food packages. Field-bred springers are lighter, wirier, built for stamina and strength, and have sparer, more feral-looking faces. The hunter in search of a springer must be absolutely certain to buy a puppy out of field stock: Show dogs rarely have the instinct, desire, or ability to hunt. Many more show-type dogs are bred than field springers, and unscrupulous breeders may imply that their dogs will hunt when in fact they will not. In the springer, as in most spaniels, hunting and show- and pet-stock dogs are all registered with the American Kennel Club (AKC).

Avoid accidentally saddling yourself with a show dog by buying from proven hunting stock. Shooting-preserve operators, professional dog trainers, and experienced hunters should know of breeders. Another way to locate a litter is to attend a spaniel hunting test, where dogs compete against a written standard rather than against one another.

An excellent route to finding a hunting springer is through an English springer spaniel field trial club: Fifty-eight of these organizations, affiliated with the AKC, are scattered across the continent. Check out a field trial, of all bird dog contests among the most realistic. A springer trial mimics actual field conditions, requiring the dogs to hunt, find, flush, and retrieve real birds. Trial people, usually hunters themselves, welcome inquiries about their dogs and customarily sell puppies to hunters. Occasionally they will have field trial rejects for sale: $750 to $1,500 for a well-trained adult dog that is too slow for the trials—and therefore a delightful hunter. One caveat: Some dogs of field trial breeding are so "hot" and hard-running that they tend to drive to the extreme edges of gun range and would not be comfortable for the average hunter to handle.

Summary: Small- to medium-size, flushes and fetches most gamebirds; especially effective on pheasants, grouse, woodcock, desert quail, and prairie grouse species in thick cover. Good for limited use on ducks; not suitable under harsh conditions. Retrieves doves. Coat requires moderate maintenance. Excellent temperament, biddable, easily and quickly trained. Widely available in good hunting lines.

Resources

The New Complete English Springer Spaniel, Charles S. Goodall and Julia Gasow. Howell Book House, New York, 1984.

"English Springer Spaniels," Jerome B. Robinson. *Sports Afield*, November 1984.

"The English Springer Spaniel," Parts I and II, Kenneth Roebuck. *Gun Dog*, November/December 1986, January/February 1987.

"Expert Opinion" (differences between show and field-bred springers), Kenneth Roebuck. *Gun Dog*, August/September 1990.

Spaniels in the Field (quarterly; covers all spaniels but emphasizes English springer), Art Rodger, ed., 10714 Escondido Dr., Cincinnati, OH 45249.

A relatively rare breed, the Welsh springer has less hunting potential than the similar English springer spaniel.

Welsh Springer
SPANIEL

T he Welsh springer is a handsome red-and-white dog that probably has been hunted for over a millennium: In 942 the laws of Howell the Good, Prince of South Wales, described a similar-sounding spaniel as a flusher for falcons and hawks. Later it plied its trade for hunters with breech-loading shotguns. Today the Welsh springer is much less well known than the English springer, yet it is still hunted in Wales, where it is known as a "starter" (for the way it starts, or flushes, game), in England, and in the United States. In the last few decades, its numbers have risen steadily on both sides of the Atlantic.

In America, most Welsh springers—"Welshies" to their owners —are pets, show dogs, or compete in obedience trials. Some, however, are hunted. A good Welsh springer will be a solid retriever, a devoted companion, and a potential candidate for the hunter seeking a versatile flushing spaniel that is a bit out of the ordinary.

Not the least of the Welsh springer's attributes is its beauty. Its

coat consists of patches of rich dark red—Irish setter red—
arrayed on the white body, usually with some ticking; the head
and ears are mostly red. The build is sturdy and muscular,
the chest deep. The cleancut head is uncomplicated with floppy
flews or overlong ears. From the tip of its docked tail to the end
of its brown nose, the Welsh springer looks every inch a worker
—"A symmetrical, compact, strong, merry, very active dog . . .
built for endurance," according to the breed standard.

The average Welsh springer is a shade smaller than its English
cousin, standing seventeen to nineteen inches at the shoulder
and weighing thirty-five to forty-five pounds, a handy size for a
gun dog or a household companion. Like the English springer, its
lustrous coat is long and heavy enough to protect against thorns,
short and light enough to be easily maintained. An oily sheen
causes mud and dirt to be quickly shed: Usually a good brushing
is all that is needed to clean the dog after a day in the field.

A Welsh springer spaniel is not simply an English springer
spaniel that comes from Wales, an assumption made by many
who are unfamiliar with the breed. The Welsh springer is a distinct breed with its own history, traits, demeanor, and appearance
—a breed in which bench and field lines have not diverged, as
they have so radically in the English springer. Some Welsh fanciers advocate shortening the breed's name to Welsh spaniel, to
more clearly separate it from the English dog.

John Phillips, a native of Wales, the author of *The Essential
Welsh Springer Spaniel*, and a man who admits he is "besotted
with Welsh springers," writes that they are gentle with children,
playful, and affectionate. Because they want and need attention,
they do not thrive in confinement—although they can spend time
in a kennel if given ample house time as well. They get along well
with other dogs. They are good watchdogs, quick to bark at suspicious noises. On the other side of the coin, if not properly

trained early in life they may become problem barkers. They tend to be reserved with strangers, but warm up if the newcomer is friendly. Like most active dogs, they need exercise daily. Writes Phillips, "If their liveliness is not channeled by some form of obedience work and supervised relationships with people, it will express itself in other ways, such as escape, destruction, and other mischief."

Welsh springers learn quickly and remember their lessons; a soft breed, they respond best to praise and encouragement. "The great gundog virtues," writes Phillips, "are docility, trainability, and readiness to serve, and [the Welsh springer spaniel] is well endowed with these." Welsh springers do require that training begin at a fairly young age: If you fail to establish control and rapport early on, the grown dog may ignore you and hunt on its own.

Most Welsh springers have excellent scenting ability. Typical of spaniels, they are natural, soft-mouthed retrievers. In covert their movements are economical and thorough. They possess great stamina and have a reputation for being able to hunt all day. They like water and are good swimmers. They hunt effectively in warm weather. Their calm nature equips them to sit and wait beside the hunter for long periods during dove or duck hunts. A good hunting Welshie will flush and fetch the gamut of upland birds.

Connie Christie, of Crozier, Virginia, has been breeding Welsh springers for seventeen years. She hunts her dogs and has handled one of her Welshies to his Senior Hunter certificate in the American Kennel Club's licensed hunting tests. She characterizes Welsh springers as "calm, tractable, thorough workers that will quarter naturally and stay within range." The average Welsh springer pup, she believes, will have at least some potential as a gun dog. "Try to pick a bold pup," she suggests.

A possible way to locate a litter (and to compare the Welsh

with the harder-hunting English springer) is to attend a spaniel hunting test. (A schedule of these events is available from the American Kennel Club.) Pockets of Welsh springer owners are scattered throughout the country. The largest group is centered in Pennsylvania, Maryland, Virginia, New Jersey, and New York. Other areas with concentrations of Welsh springers are Wisconsin and northern Illinois; Georgia and Florida; Phoenix, Arizona; and California.

In 1990, a total of 268 Welsh springers were registered with the AKC, compared to over 20,000 English springers. Although most of the English were of show or pet stock and essentially useless as hunters, a good many were of field trial or hunting blood, making it far easier to find a hunting prospect within the English breed. While few Welsh springers possess the hard-driving intensity and strong hunting instinct of a good field-bred English springer, the Welsh spaniel offers a choice for a different sort of spaniel gun dog—slower, perhaps easier to train, perhaps more thorough and apt to stick closer to its human partner.

Summary: Small- to medium-size; thorough worker suited to most upland gamebirds in thick cover. Retrieves. Coat requires moderate upkeep. Good temperament; best housed indoors. Less widely available in hunting bloodlines, and a much chancier prospect, than the similar English springer spaniel.

Resources

The Welsh Springer Spaniel, William Pferd III. A. S. Barnes, South Brunswick, N. J., 1977.

The Essential Welsh Springer Spaniel, John Phillips. Stanhope Press, Chelmsford, England, 1985.

"The Welsh Springer Spaniel," James B. Spencer. *Gun Dog*, June/July 1990.

Welsh Springer Spaniel Club of America: Susan Riese, 2346 Corinth-Poseyville Rd., Bremen, GA 30110.

The English cocker spaniel, if from hunting lines, can be an excellent flush dog, especially on woodcock. (The American cocker, not pictured, has almost vanished as a hunting breed.)

Cocker
SPANIEL

I n *The American Sportsman,* in 1884, Elisha J. Lewis wrote concerning dogs used for woodcock: "Cockers, from their size, are much better adapted by nature to the pursuit of this game than either the setter or pointer, which latter cannot insinuate themselves into the recesses of our briery coverts."

"Cocker," a form of the word "'cocking," refers to a small English spaniel whose size made it a good choice for hunting 'cock—woodcock. Up until this century, the cocker was actually the same breed as the springer. The bigger dogs were called springers and were used to spring larger game, while the smaller cockers, weighing under twenty-five pounds, were hunted preferentially on the Eurasian woodcock, which, like its North American counterpart, is often found in thick places better negotiated by a smaller dog.

In America, the cocker spaniel was a popular hunter during the eighteenth and nineteenth centuries. In the twentieth century, hunters and field trialers turned more to other spaniel breeds, especially the English springer. Far from dying out, the cocker caught on as a show dog and a pet: From 1936 through 1952, and again from 1983 to the present day, more cocker spaniels were registered with the American Kennel Club than any other breed. A blending of several spaniel strains gave rise to what is currently called the American cocker: a small dog whose "cute" features have been emphasized through selective breeding. With few exceptions, today's American cocker (105,000 registered in 1990, making it the most popular breed in the nation) is unfit for the field. Its long, silken fur would soon become matted with stick-tights, its bulbous eyes would be scratched by brush, and its pendulous ears would snag on briars. Its hunting instincts are dim to nonexistent.

Many hunters say that the American cocker has been ruined by bench breeding and inflated production for the pet market. This hardly makes sense. If a core of devoted breeders had kept producing good gun dogs, two separate strains—field and bench—would have diverged, as has happened with the English springer. But the old-line cocker breeders stopped; they retired, or died, and were replaced by a new generation that liked the springer better. A popular book published in 1967, *Hunting Dogs*, by Philip Rice and John Dahl, states: "The cocker spaniel has no real advantages over the English springer. . . . The cocker is not as fast as the springer and generally not as effective in flushing upland game."

The operative word in the preceding quotation is "fast." As cities expanded, hunting cover was erased and gamebirds dwindled; many hunters turned to field trials as a new way of connecting with their dogs and the outdoors. In a spaniel trial, the fast, stylish dog is rewarded over the slower, more methodical worker. In America, most trials are held in fields where the cover is light enough that the judges can observe the dogs. But under actual hunting conditions—in a riot of thornapples, a briar-choked bottom, a stiff stand of pencil popple—a slower dog may actually cover more of the habitat than a faster dog, and, by keeping the action closer to the gun, give the hunter more time to get off a shot. In 1842, in *Recreations in Shooting*, the British author Craven wrote of cockers: "If taught to keep always within half a gunshot, they are the best dogs in existence."

The last Cocker National Field Championship was held in 1962, the last licensed trial for cockers in 1965. Since 1946, the American Kennel Club has recognized two separate breeds of cocker, the American and the English. The English looks less a caricature of its former hunting self—although the vast majority of the English cockers in the United States are from bench strains, and are unlikely to make good hunters.

The 1970s saw a resurgence of the hunting cocker, a trend that continues to this day. One of the leaders of the movement is Vance Van Laanen, a hunter and dog fancier who owns a small steel mill in Green Bay, Wisconsin. While shopping for a springer spaniel in 1977, Van Laanen saw a pair of English cockers owned by a Scottish gamekeeper working on an estate in Wisconsin. As the story goes, Van Laanen committed the indiscretion of doubting the hunting ability of another man's dogs, whereupon the Scotsman went to the kennel's tack room, got out two shotguns and tossed one to Van Laanen, went to the pheasant pen, extracted two pheasants, released them in a nearby field, and turned his cockers loose.

The Scotsman tooted on his whistle, the cockers hupped. He cast them off, and they began quartering down the field. When the dogs flushed a pheasant, the Scotsman whistled again and both dogs sat: Van Laanen shot the pheasant, the Scotsman released one of the dogs by calling its name, and the appointed cocker raced to the bird and fetched it. Van Laanen was sold.

A year later, Van Laanen went to Scotland and bought two English cockers out of working stock. They turned out to be excellent grouse and woodcock dogs in the dense aspen and tag alders of northern Wisconsin. Their peppy, enthusiastic manner further charmed Van Laanen, who imported other English cockers and began breeding them. Today he is linked to a young couple, Stan and Lisa Wrobel, professional gun dog trainers in Greenleaf, Wisconsin. The Wrobels train many of the pups Van Laanen sells to local hunters, and have begun importing field-bred cockers from Great Britain for their own breeding program. As well as the Wrobels, several other kennels in the United States breed and sell hunting strains of English cockers. Periodically, litters are advertised in the magazines *Spaniels in the Field* and *Gun Dog*.

The hunting cocker weighs twenty to twenty-five pounds. Colors may be liver-and-white, black-and-white, blue roan (a mixture of blue-gray and white), lemon-and-white, solid liver, or solid black. The coat is thick but not flossy. The tail is docked.

The hunting English cocker has a calm, settled disposition that makes it a pleasant house dog, even in the close quarters of an apartment. It is good with children. Temperament is much like that of the springer: affectionate, intelligent, and anxious to please, except that the cocker may display a bit more individuality and stubbornness and a tendency toward mischievousness. Some cockers are said to require "considerably more patience on the part of the trainer." The cocker develops an extremely close bond with its owner; this, in turn, contributes to the dog's tendency and willingness to stay close to its master in the field.

While cockers can certainly handle ring-necked pheasants, the larger, stronger springer will do a more consistent job on these big, tough birds. Cockers can retrieve ducks from water—but again, the springer has the size and toughness to do a better job. The game on which cockers excel is, of course, the game for which they are named: woodcock. Also, their naturally close range and excellent powers of scent make them quite effective on ruffed grouse. A cocker may not cover as much ground in the open field as a springer will, but it will worm under brush and canes that a springer would have to breast, thereby keeping its nose closer to the ground to pick up foot scent. As is true of most spaniels, cockers are instinctive, soft-mouthed retrievers.

"The spaniel naturally gives tongue on his scent the moment he strikes it," wrote Frank Forester of cockers in the mid-1800s, "hunts it up with the rapidity of light, and springs his bird or starts his hare with a rush. By education he is made to hunt mute ... and to give tongue only when it is flushed." That sharp, excited bark told the hunter, *Get ready to shoot!* Today's cockers apparently no longer possess this useful trait.

The English cocker is nowhere a common dog. It is a minor breed in Britain, used on rough shoots (where hunters ramble through woods, fields, and marshes, taking whatever game is encountered) and as a nonslip retriever on driven game. There are cocker spaniel field trials in Britain, none in North America. In the last decade of the twentieth century, it is hard to say how many hunting English cockers exist in the United States. Van Laanen estimates five hundred to six hundred; others put the number closer to two thousand.

The biggest disadvantage of the hunting cocker spaniel is that there are so few of them around. You could run up a considerable telephone bill finding a litter; and you might end up having to order a dog sight unseen, rather a leap of faith but perhaps worth the risk if you are an apartment-bound hunter, or if you are simply charmed by these handsome, diminutive dogs.

Summary: Small flushing spaniel most useful on woodcock and grouse; also works on pheasants. Good retriever. Friendly, merry, occasionally mischievous. Well suited to living indoors. The English cocker is a better prospect than the American, although both are hard to find in actual field breeding.

Resources

"The Return of the Hunting Cocker Spaniel," Charles Frisk. *Spaniels in the Field*, Fall 1990.

"The Hunting Cocker Spaniel," Jerome B. Robinson. *Sports Afield*, November 1989.

"The Cocker Congregation," Larry Mueller. *Outdoor Life*, March 1990.

"A Merry American Revival," Larry Mueller. *Outdoor Life*, August 1990.

American Water
SPANIEL

N ot too big, not too small; a good worker on ruffed grouse, woodcock, pheasants, shorebirds; an excellent swimmer and retriever of waterfowl, at home in a canoe or a skiff; friendly, cheerful, tractable, intelligent, American born and bred: Shouldn't such a dog be hunted coast to coast?

Probably the main reason the American water spaniel has never really caught on is that most people do not think it a handsome dog. Too, it has a curly coat that picks up burs and sticktights in the uplands. Over the last decade around 300 American water spaniels have been registered annually by the American Kennel Club, ranking it somewhere around 100 out of 130 recognized breeds. But if the American has never found wide popularity, it has nevertheless persisted as a respected, versatile gun dog since its emergence in the upper Midwest some time before the Civil War.

The American water spaniel was developed in the swampy, river-laced region of east-central Wisconsin as an all-around up-

A close-working flusher and fetcher of ducks and upland game, the American water spaniel is most common in the upper Midwest.

land hunter and duck dog. Several theories explain the breed's genesis. Settlers in the area took local Indian hunting dogs, and possibly the old English water spaniel (now extinct as a breed), and, to make a hardier, longer-legged dog, crossed these with Irish water spaniels and curly-coated retrievers. Or, the field spaniel was crossed with the curly-coated retriever.

The American water spaniel stands fifteen to twenty inches at the shoulders and weighs thirty to forty-five pounds—about the size of an English springer. The build is sturdy, compact, sometimes a bit long in the body. The water-shedding, bur-attracting coat is curled, dense, and dark liver in color. The deep brown eyes are set on a line with the top of the ears; the forehead is broad, smooth, and flat, lacking the Irish water spaniel's pronounced poodle-like topknot. The fur is short on the face. The tail, which is never docked, is bowed, or rocker-shaped, and covered with curly hair. The overall effect is utilitarian.

A small-town doctor, F. J. Pfeifer, of New London, Wisconsin, is credited with having done the most to improve and stabilize the breed. In the 1920s his Wolf River Kennels housed upwards of 130 American water spaniels and sold over 100 puppies a year, shipping them as far away as Texas and Louisiana. Pfeifer charged twenty dollars for females, twenty-five dollars for males, and offered an unconditional money-back guarantee, which, it is said, not a single buyer ever used. Around the same time, when demand for the dogs was high, other kennels sprang up, most of them in Wisconsin and neighboring states. In 1938 the Field Dog Stud Book recognized the American water spaniel as a distinct breed; two years later, the American Kennel Club followed suit.

The American water spaniel can be readily taught to quarter before the gun. It has a good sense of smell. On dry land the average American water spaniel will hunt as well as, or better than, most Labrador and golden retrievers. Its hunting manner will be less spirited and brisk than that of the typical English springer, making it comfortable to hunt behind at a walking pace.

David Duffey, a Wisconsin native and a respected modern writer about dogs, has owned, trained, and hunted with more than a dozen American water spaniels. He characterizes the breed as a busy, sure worker that tends to stay close to the gun. Duffey's Americans, he writes, have been "particularly adept at flushing ruffed grouse, woodcock, and pheasant, as well as being nonslip retrievers for dove and ducks or when jump-shooting waterfowl." The American water spaniel will handle all normal duck-retrieving chores. Duffey notes that a crippled Canada goose can be tough for an American to subdue and retrieve, but that only the Chesapeake Bay retriever or Irish water spaniel will do a better job. Although not a fast swimmer, the American is persistent and less affected by the cold than any other spaniel except the Irish water spaniel, which is usually classed with the retrievers.

The breed is used effectively on quail, sharp-tailed grouse, prairie chicken, and Hungarian partridge when these open-country birds resort to thickets. (Some Americans will point a bird that sits tight, a trait that can be encouraged during training.) It will work sora, rails, and jacksnipe. It will do a good job on furred game, starting rabbits and retrieving them, and even treeing squirrels.

According to Duffey, the American water spaniel has a sharper temperament than the ingratiating, eager-to-please nature of most other spaniels. A quick learner with good retention, the American may, however, balk and show resentment if pushed to do something it does not want to do. Still, Duffey insists, "Training can be undertaken by an amateur whose time, facilities, and talents are limited." American water spaniels are natural retrievers when started on play-fetching right after weaning. They exhibit hunting ability at an early age. The breed is companionable, has a loving disposition, and is good around children. It may tend toward protectiveness, devotion to one person, and suspicion of strangers, traits which, combined with toughness in the field, lead Duffey to conclude that the American "might be considered the Chesapeake among spaniels."

The breed has always been known for its adaptable, communicative nature and ability to figure things out on its own. A story in *Hunting Dog* magazine, by a Wisconsinite named Lloyd Bare, blends rural humor and the water spaniel's reputation for intelligence:

"I can remember when I was a small boy, my grandfather showing off his American, 'Brownie,' in our family drug store. Before Grandpa's cronies came in, he would line up his morning's bag in the back room. Very often he would have three or four different kinds of ducks after a morning's hunt. He would line them up in the order that he planned to call for them. When his friends came in, he would tell them what a smart dog he had and what a good retriever he was. 'In fact, he's so smart he can identify different species,' Grandpa would say. With that he would say, 'Brownie, go get the mallard,' and sure enough Brownie would go to the back room and come back with the mallard. This would go on until each duck had been brought out, in the order that Grandpa called for them."

Who uses the breed today? Farmers, trappers, mixed-bag hunters who refuse to limit themselves to any one sort of game. By far, most American water spaniels are produced and hunted in Wisconsin (where the breed is the state dog), Minnesota, and Michigan, with a few in New England and elsewhere; the American is probably our most regional breed. A disadvantage in choosing an American water spaniel is that unless you live in or near the upper Midwest, you will almost certainly have a hard time actually seeing a litter and picking an individual pup. On the other hand, you will not have to worry as much about accidentally getting a dog out of show stock, because the American's appearance has never made it a popular candidate for the bench. Most issues of *Gun Dog* magazine carry advertisements for American water spaniels.

Duffey cites several reasons why the American has never become widely popular and probably never will. Stiff competition from the Labrador retriever and English springer spaniel, both of which can do as much in the field and are considered better-looking; no field trials to showcase the breed's talents; no well-financed, high-profile breeding programs. "His sole credential for existence," Duffey concludes, "is his performance as an honest hunting dog."

Summary: Medium-size flushing breed good on grouse, woodcock, pheasants, shorebirds; slower hunting pace than English springer; excellent retriever of waterfowl, including geese. Coat picks up burs. Loving disposition, although may become protective of owner and family. Quick learner. Very much a hunting breed, with little show or pet influence. Few breeders located outside of upper Midwest.

Resources

"Born and Bred in the U. S. A.," Dave Duffey. *Gun Dog*, May/June 1987.

American Water Spaniel Club: P.O. Box 1535, Sheboygen, WI 53082.

Boykin SPANIEL

Alec White strolled down Main Street. He was running a few minutes late—but then it was such a fine South Carolina Sunday, the sky clear, the air crisp, cardinals whistling. He heard the piano starting up in First Presbyterian, the voices rising for the hymn, and quickened his pace.

He realized that someone was following him. He stopped and turned. A brown dog, half-grown, stood a few feet off. A sturdy, handy-looking little fellow. A stray? White lowered himself to a crouch. "Here, boy." The dog, tail low and wagging, came up to sniff White's hand. "Smell my dogs, don't you?" White scratched behind a brown, floppy ear. "You lost?"

The dog's tail sped up. The singing in the church had stopped;

The Boykin spaniel, a Southern breed, excels on doves, ducks, turkeys, and the gamut of upland birds.

White knew his family would be waiting and his wife wouldn't like it, him coming in late. He straightened, turned, strode to the church steps, stopped and glanced back. The dog, still watching him, had sat down in the grass. A brainy-looking fellow, with those keen yellow eyes. Probably some hunt in him, too; looked like he had spaniel blood. Well. White smiled and shrugged, went inside.

When he came out again an hour later, the dog was still there.

It's supposed to have happened more or less that way, on the Sunday in 1908, or perhaps 1909, when Alec White became attached to a nondescript stray that eventually gave rise to a whole breed of hunting dogs. White's new dog, which he named Dumpy, soon became his favorite, a solid retriever of ducks, more convenient in a small boat and more agile than White's Chesapeakes, and a good turkey dog besides. Dumpy was sent to White's lifelong friend and hunting partner, Whit Boykin, owner of Pine Grove plantation, about ten miles from Camden, South Carolina. There Dumpy was mated to another brown dog of equally uncertain lineage (said to have been left unclaimed at the railroad station), and the Boykin spaniel was born. The breed is renowned today for its energy, fetching and scenting skills, trainability, and engaging personality.

The Boykin spaniel was developed mainly by Whit Boykin and his descendents. Although no kennel records exist, crosses were reputedly made with English springers, pointers, Chesapeake Bay retrievers, and American water spaniels. Some authorities surmise that the original Boykin, Dumpy, was himself an American water spaniel.

The modern Boykin is a bit smaller than the English springer, standing fourteen to eighteen inches at the shoulder and weighing twenty-five to forty pounds. The Boykin has the typical spaniel profile and conformation: fairly short legs, a sturdy body, a domed head, soulful eyes, and thick floppy ears. The tail is docked to about three inches. There is a good deal of latitude in the breed standard for the coat: anything from short and straight to medium-length and curly, preferably with light feathering on the legs. The Boykin is colored a solid rich liver or dark chocolate, although sunlight may bleach the fur to a reddish hue. The eyes, set well apart, are dark yellow to brown.

Early Boykins were used primarily as turkey dogs. They would work back and forth along an advancing line of hunters, flushing turkeys ahead to other gunners lying in wait. Or they were employed as "still hunters," a use that ultimately led to the practice of docking the dog's tail. As explained in "America's Third Dog," an article by Richard Wolters: "The hunter and his Boykin walked through a likely patch until the dog found the scent and flushed the birds in every direction. Once the birds were scattered, the hunter built himself a small blind. . . . Man and dog had to stay hidden, motionless and absolutely silent except for the turkey-calling device that enticed the birds back. . . . Hunters could teach the dog to sit quietly and watch the birds coming back into gun range, but they could not stop that excited tail from wagging. There was not enough room in a blind for man, dog, and a swishing tail that rustled every twig and leaf within reach. Off came the tail."

The Boykin quarters briskly in front of the gun and can be used to flush virtually any upland bird—woodcock, grouse, pheasant, partridge, quail, turkey. It is a close-working, medium-speed hunter. In the South, where the breed is most plentiful, the Boykin is often used as a "wagon dog"; it rides on a mule-drawn wagon, and from this vantage point marks down quail that have been shot over setters or pointers. The Boykin is then sent to fetch, often making multiple retrieves, returning and dropping each bird into a box mounted on the wagon.

Boykins are known for their stamina. Strong swimmers and retrievers, they will fetch ducks from open water or marsh. Boykins are too small to handle geese easily; one of the retriever breeds is a better choice for goose hunting and for working under frigid conditions. But the Boykin's diminutiveness offers certain advantages: The dog can ride in a small skiff or a canoe, and can jump overboard without tipping the craft; returning, it can be grabbed by the scruff of the neck and hauled back into the boat, duck and all.

Boykins withstand the heat that accompanies September dove seasons in the South. Hunters often set their Boykins facing them, so that the dog can watch the sky behind, while the master covers the front. The dog alerts the gunner to incoming birds by wagging its (albeit abbreviated) tail.

Boykins are exuberant, alert, intelligent, and likeable. They thrive on affection and are far happier in the house than the kennel. They respond to a light hand in training. According to August Watkins, of Middleburg, Virginia, who is on the Board of Directors of the Boykin Spaniel Society, "Boykins are easily trained. They can actually be taught to point. They're such amenable dogs they can be taught almost any hunting task."

The Boykin spaniel is one of only four breeds developed solely in North America. (The others are the American water spaniel, Chesapeake Bay retriever, and Nova Scotia duck tolling retriever.) South Carolina remains the center for Boykin breeding, where the breed is the state dog. However, the Boykin has been widely exported, with approximately seven thousand registered nationwide with the Boykin Spaniel Society. By comparison, over twenty thousand English springer spaniels were registered with the American Kennel Club in 1990 alone—some as hunters, some as field trial dogs, and the majority as nonhunting pet or show dogs. Apparently, most owners of Boykin spaniels have little or no desire to show their dogs. In the article by Richard Wolters, Dr. Peter McKoy, a Camden veterinarian and a founder of the Boykin Spaniel Society, is quoted as saying: "We do not want the Boykin recognized by the American Kennel Club. We have seen hunting breeds that, after being bred for conformation, lose entirely their hunting instinct as they become pretty show dogs—for example, the poodle, the cocker spaniel, the Irish and English setters."

Today a significant health problem is affecting the Boykin, as well as other hunting breeds. Canine hip dysplasia (CHD) is an inherited condition in which the hip joint degenerates, leading to pain and crippling. Dysplasia is often exacerbated in hard-driving hunting dogs who literally wear out their hips charging through cover, retrieving, and doing other strenuous work. CHD can be detected on an X-ray photograph. The malady tends not to show up until a dog is two to three years old. Anyone buying a mature dog should have the animal's hips radiographed and examined by a veterinarian. A person seeking a Boykin puppy would be wise to buy from stock that has been certified CHD-free, and to obtain a written contract from the breeder allowing a refund or a replacement puppy if the dog develops CHD.

Once a year the Boykin Spaniel Society holds its own national field trial (actually more of a hunting test) in Camden, South Carolina. To learn about litters, check the classified ads in *Gun Dog* magazine or the newsletter of the Boykin Spaniel Society.

Summary: Small- to medium-size gun dog. Flushes and fetches all upland birds. Excellent retriever and dove dog. Fetches ducks from water, although not suited to cold, harsh conditions. Withstands heat well. Friendly, highly trainable. Available in good hunting lines; canine hip dysplasia a problem in some dogs. Most breeders located in South.

Resources

"America's Third Dog," Richard Wolters. *Connoisseur*, October 1988.

"Boykin—An American Original," Joe Arnette. *Gun Dog*, September 1989.

The Boykin Spaniel Society: P.O. Box 2047, Camden, SC, 29020.

The stocky, heavy Clumber spaniel is slow afield, with an excellent nose. Although most are bred for pets or the show ring, many will hunt.

Clumber
SPANIEL

Were it not for the French Revolution, an English duke, a tenacious gamekeeper, and a cadre of show breeders, there might be no Clumber spaniel hunting today. In fact, the breed barely exists: In 1989 only 78 Clumbers were registered with the American Kennel Club and 182 with the English Kennel Club. The Clumber survives essentially as a show dog, but its hunting instincts are so deeply entrenched that they can often be brought to the fore simply by introducing the dog to game.

The Clumber is a stocky, heavy dog, mostly white in color, slow afield, a reliable game finder with an exceptional nose. James Farrow, in his book *The Clumber Spaniel*, published in 1912, wrote: "Speaking generally, the Clumber is not an active Spaniel; he is far too heavy in bone and construction for that. . . . On the other hand, he has plenty of pluck and endurance, and will stand a heavy day's work . . . pushing stuff out of thick cover."

Legend has it that an elderly French nobleman, the Duc de Noailles, decided on the eve of the French Revolution to give away his kennel of spaniels. The dogs were shipped across the English Channel, going from Duc to Duke: the beneficiary being the Duke of Newcastle, whose manor, Clumber Park, was in Sherwood Forest. To the Duke of Newcastle's gamekeeper, William Mansell, goes the credit for developing the breed as a well-rounded hunting dog. The nineteenth-century British writer Stonehenge, in his *Manual of Rural Sports*, wrote: "The Clumber spaniel is the best I have ever seen, being hardy and capable of braving wet with impunity. His nose is also wonderfully good, which its full development in point of size would lead one to expect. They are bred so much for hunting cock [woodcock] that they own the scent very readily, and seem to delight and revel in it."

In 1972, C. Bede Maxwell wrote in *The Truth About Sporting Dogs:* "The high tide of Clumber fashion [came] when British royalty hunted over the spaniels, and these were fostered in the Sandringham Kennels that were the pride of King Edward VII. His father, Prince Albert, the Consort of Queen Victoria, had been first to introduce the spaniels, and in turn his son, King George V, a dedicated sportsman and superb shot, used them too. King George's Clumbers were not permitted to retrieve: for this service only Labradors were used."

The Clumber reached North America in the mid-1800s and became fairly popular. Henry William Herbert, a transplanted Briton and the foremost American outdoor writer of his day, praised Clumbers as "unwearied and dauntless dogs." The Clumber spaniel was one of ten original breeds recognized by the fledgling American Kennel Club in 1884. When spaniel field trials began in 1899, Clumbers dominated for several years. But tastes changed, field trialers opted for faster, more biddable English springers, hunters followed suit, and the number of Clumbers declined. Today, however, many feel the breed is ready to stage a comeback.

The modern Clumber stands seventeen to nineteen inches at the withers and weighs sixty to eighty-five pounds—the height of a springer and the weight of a Labrador. The coat is white, with patches of yellow or orange, mainly on the ears and head. The head is ponderous, the nose pink. The deep-set eyes show pronounced "haw" (the pinkish inner membrane); the heavy flews and fleshy, stolid physiognomy have prompted some observers to liken the Clumber's face to that of Sir Winston Churchill.

The coat consists of long, fairly coarse outer guard hairs over a shorter, insulating, water-resistant inner coat. Burs and mud are not particularly a problem.

It is a nice coincidence that "Clumber" suggests the verb "lumber," because that is how this massive spaniel moves. The Clumber's powerful body helps it plow through heavy cover; its short legs let it crawl beneath dense brush and serve to keep it within gun range even when it is hot on the trail. The Clumber hunts at a steady, resolute pace, its nose to the ground. It does not flush its birds with the headlong abandon of an English springer, but instead slows down as it approaches the quarry and detects body scent, homes in on the target, and makes a final lunge—the slow approach giving the hunter ample time to get ready for the shot. Another basic difference between the springer and the Clumber is that the Clumber tracks naturally and must be taught to quarter, while the springer quarters naturally and must be taught to track.

The Clumber is best used on game that resorts to dense cover: ruffed grouse, woodcock, pheasant. Its slow pace is an advantage in the thickest covers, where thoroughness may be more important than speed. Most Clumbers are good swimmers and retrieve readily from streams and lakes. The breed's outstanding nose and relentless nature make it an effective trailer of wounded ducks in the marsh.

Darrell Reeves, a forester living in Oregon, is field chairman for the Clumber Spaniel Club of America. He probably has more experience training and hunting Clumbers than anyone else in the nation. Reeves hunts his Clumbers on pheasants, ruffed grouse, and mountain quail. Mountain quail are covey birds: The covey tends to run ahead of a pursuing dog, with individual birds splitting off from the group and hiding. A fast spaniel, Reeves contends, misses these skulking singles; his Clumbers' more leisurely pace lets them pick up on the skulkers, and does not flush the rest of the covey wild. Reeves believes the Clumber picks up faint scent better than most other dogs. He refers to the breed as "the ultimate meat dog."

According to Reeves, all Clumbers today exist as a result of show breeding. "The breed comes from a very small gene pool that was originally bred as hunters," he says. "The instinct to hunt is so strong that you probably couldn't eradicate it even if you wanted to." Reeves has tried Clumbers out of every major show line in the United States, and, he reports, "Basically you have as good a chance of getting a birdy pup out of one line as the next." He estimates that eighty-five to ninety percent of Clumber pups have the potential to become hunters, with fifty percent becoming "very good, solid dogs"; however, ten to fifteen percent "won't care about birds at all."

Reeves characterizes the Clumber as "a big dog that's placid inside the house. It sleeps a lot. About ninety-eight percent of them snore." The Clumber is not aware or alert enough to make a good watchdog: "A Clumber will bark at a stranger," notes Reeves, "if it happens to wake up."

Clumbers tend to be conservative and stubborn. Lacking the ingratiating enthusiasm of a springer spaniel, they do not always find it necessary to please their masters. But, says Reeves, "I've taken a lot of my Clumbers out hunting after only ten hours of training. I introduce them to pigeons and gunfire, make buddies of them, and teach general obedience. They produce birds with a minimum of training."

The Clumber has a reputation for occasionally tuning out its master, and, absorbed in the olfactory surroundings, plodding along like a basset hound trailing a rabbit—hardly a problem for the hunter, who simply follows until the dog catches up to the quarry and flushes it. Each year, more and more Clumbers are being entered in hunting tests, where a dog competes against a written standard rather than against other dogs. The Clumber Spaniel Club of America—primarily a bench organization—sponsors a hunting test as part of its national get-together each year.

Clumbers typically have small litters—about four pups—and only twenty-four litters were registered in the United States in 1990. Darrell Reeves and his wife, Jane, sell ten to fifteen puppies a year to hunters, about half the dogs they produce. According to Reeves, most breeders have a waiting list, and some refuse to sell to hunters because the dog will not be shown. Other breeders may want to co-own female pups to exercise control over breeding.

Summary: Large, low-slung, powerful, slow afoot. Good worker on grouse, woodcock, pheasant, mountain quail in thickest cover. Sure tracker and retriever. Requires little training. Poor watchdog; the longish white coat is shed year-round. A traditional hunting breed, now rare; may be available only from show stock.

Resources

"The Clumber Spaniel," Kenneth Roebuck. *Gun Dog,* July/August 1983.

"The Clumber Spaniel, the Mellow Hunter's Helper," James B. Spencer. *Gun Dog*, November/December 1988.

Darrell Reeves, Field Chairman, Clumber Spaniel Club of America: 9731 Hubbard Creek Rd., Umpqua, OR 97486.

Field and Sussex
SPANIELS

L ike the Clumber spaniel, today's field and Sussex spaniels are essentially show dogs that retain at least some of their ancestral hunting ardor and ability. They are rare breeds. According to the American Kennel Club, in 1990 only seventy-seven field spaniels (in twenty-eight litters) and forty-three Sussex (in eleven litters) were registered throughout the country. The breeds are only slightly more popular in England.

The field spaniel was developed originally as a bench breed. In the nineteenth century, dog fanciers among the British nobility and economic aristocracy took various land spaniels and fashioned a large, low, stocky black spaniel that became, briefly, the darling of the show ring. When trained for hunting (most people who showed dogs at that time also hunted with them), the field spaniel was found to have an excellent nose and good endurance, but was frequently headstrong, hard to train, and disinclined to retrieve.

The field spaniel almost vanished in the twentieth century. In

Field and Sussex spaniels are mainly show dogs with limited hunting potential. Above, this young field will become stockier as he matures. Below, a Sussex puzzles out a trail.

the 1960s, breeders in England crossed the few remaining individuals with English springers—again to create a show dog, this one with longer legs. But since the choice for outbreeding was a strong hunting variety, what resulted was a spaniel that could, coincidentally, hunt.

Unlike the first edition of the breed, the modern field spaniel has a soft, affectionate temperament. It is playful, slow to mature, friendly toward other dogs, good with children, active and energetic around the house. Intelligent and eager to please, the field spaniel requires ongoing training—as much to occupy the dog's active mind as to maintain a proper deportment. The breed would rather live indoors, close to its humans, than in a kennel. Field spaniel owners report that their dogs are prodigious snorers.

The field spaniel stands about eighteen inches and weighs forty-five to fifty-five pounds. It is lower and heavier-boned than the English springer, taller and less ponderous than the Clumber. The body, according to the breed standard, is "somewhat longer than tall," but not as attenuated as that of the Clumber. The field spaniel has sturdy legs and large, broad feet. The tail is docked "to balance the overall dog." The field spaniel looks like (and is) a strong, muscular canine with good endurance.

The breed's head has been described as "well-chiseled." It resembles that of an Irish setter or a field-type English setter. The nose is large and fleshy, the ears long and dangling, the muzzle long and lean and without excessive dewlaps. The eyes are dark hazel to deep brown.

The coat is flat or wavy, dense, and water-repellent. Feathering adorns the chest, underbody, legs, and tail. Field spaniels come in several beautiful colors: black, chocolate, liver, light gold, roan.

Hunting, the field spaniel has a moderate pace—slower than the English springer, faster than the Clumber; about the same as the Welsh springer spaniel, according to James B. Spencer, writing in *Gun Dog* magazine. They may be used on all upland birds.

Their proponents claim that field spaniels are easily taught to hup (sit) at the flushing of a bird or a gunshot, and to work close to the hunter, making them suitable for small patches of thick cover near developed areas. Field spaniels are reputed to be good retrievers and swimmers, and to have the typically excellent spaniel nose.

Writes Peggy Grayson in *The History and Management of the Field Spaniel:* "Those shooting men who have purchased and trained fields over the past ten years are all loud in their praise for the breed's working capabilities, and more enquiries for working stock, or puppies likely to make good workers, come each year." According to James Spencer, "This country is full of hunters who would be happier with field spaniels than with any other dog—if they just knew about the breed."

Peggy Grayson is also the author of *The Sussex Spaniel.* The Sussex's origin, writes Grayson, "lies in the fast-vanishing countryside of southern England, where it was originally bred to work the difficult heavy clay terrain of Kent and Sussex [counties]. Together with cocker and field spaniels, the Sussex spaniel can be traced back to common mid-nineteenth-century forebears."

The Sussex is long, low, and level. Typically it stands about fifteen inches and weighs thirty-five to forty-five pounds—about the same weight as an English springer but several inches shorter and somewhat longer. The Sussex's compact, muscular form is geared toward strength and stamina rather than agility and speed.

The Sussex has a double coat, a coarse outer layer over a shorter, insulating inner one. Ears, legs, and tail are moderately feathered. The fur is an overall rich golden brown. The lowset ears are large, the brow heavy, the blunt, squared muzzle adorned with heavy flews. The eyes are hazel and the nose liver-colored. The tail is docked so that in the mature dog it is five to seven inches long.

The Sussex has been characterized as a "merry" dog that thrives in its master's house and languishes in a kennel. Like the Clumber spaniel, the Sussex sleeps much of the day. Yet in contrast to its sedentary nature, the Sussex is often protective and territorial. It tends to be aggressive toward other dogs and will defend its home turf against strange humans.

Most observers do not attribute high intelligence to the breed. Some Sussex can be stubborn, requiring patience and a light hand in training. Many hunters simply teach basic obedience commands, then turn their dogs loose in good game cover and follow along with shotguns ready.

Historically, the Sussex hunted pheasant, partridge, duck, woodcock, snipe, and hare. The Sussex tends to work slowly and close to the gun. Often a Sussex will show instinctive ability to search and trail. In covert, it will worm under brush that another dog would have to drive through or leap over, thus keeping its nose close to foot scent on the ground. The occasional Sussex will give tongue, or bark, when it flushes a bird. The breed is tenacious and has good stamina. Natural retrieving instincts vary. Some Sussex fetch readily from land and water; others simply sniff out a dead bird and stand over it, waiting for the hunter to pick it up.

According to Larry Mueller, writing in *Outdoor Life*, the small Sussex gene pool has created breeding problems. Some females have difficulty conceiving, and "pup survival is not the best. An average of four pups survive from a litter of five or six."

The major obstacles to hunting with either a Sussex or a field spaniel are locating a litter, determining whether the pups' immediate ancestors have any hunting potential, and being resigned to the fact that your pup will have a much higher probability of being a poor bird dog than will a puppy out of another spaniel breed with stronger hunting instincts. There have been several recent articles in outdoor magazines on Sussex and field spaniels; one suspects that the writers, in looking for something differ-ent to report on, are describing too liberally the hunting abilities of these dwindling show-stock breeds.

Summary: Large, heavy-boned, low-slung dogs; work thick cover for upland birds. Field spaniel seems to have more hunting poten-tial than Sussex, although Clumber has more potential than ei-ther. Field and Sussex now limited to show stock, extremely rare, and a poor choice for beginning trainer. Sussex spaniels may be aggressively protective.

Resources

The History and Management of the Field Spaniel, Peggy Grayson. Scan Books, Brighton, England, 1984.

"The Field Spaniel," James B. Spencer. *Gun Dog,* October/November 1990.

The Sussex Spaniel, Peggy Grayson. Boydell Press, Wood-bridge, England, 1989.

"The Sussex Spaniel," James B. Spencer. *Gun Dog,* December 1990/January 1991.

"A Rare Breed," (Sussex spaniel) Larry Mueller. *Outdoor Life,* March 1991.

II

RETRIEVERS

---

*The duck and the dog were so
far away that by the time
Blue caught the scoter, we
couldn't be sure the mirac-
ulous event had occurred except that the dog appeared to
be swimming back.*

—GEORGE REIGER
The Wildfowler's Quest

The Englishman Nicholas Cox wrote in 1674 in *The Gentleman's Recreation:* "There are two sorts of [spaniels] which
necessarily serve for Fowling. The first findeth Game on the
Land, the other on the Water. . . . The Spaniel, whose service is
required in Fowling on the Water, partly through natural inclination and partly by diligently teaching, is properly called Aquat-
icus, [or] Water-Spaniel. . . . His size is somewhat big, and of a
measurable greatness, having long, rough, and curled hair. . . .
Ducks and Drakes are his principal Game."

In England the spaniels—dogs whose ancestors originally

came from Spain—were at one time, as Cox tells us, divided into two classes. The original water spaniels contributed greatly to the seven retriever breeds commonly used in North America today: Labrador retriever, golden retriever, Irish water spaniel, curly-coated retriever, and flat-coated retriever, which all come directly from Britain; and the Chesapeake Bay retriever and Nova Scotia duck tolling retriever, developed in America from stock of British origin.

As the name implies, the chief function of a retriever is to bring back game after the hunter has killed or wounded it. It is a sobering fact that a certain percentage of birds are wounded and then lost: One writer estimates ten to fifteen percent go unrecovered even when a dog is on hand to fetch; the figure soars to forty to sixty percent when a dog is not employed. Retrievers will fetch from marsh, open water, or dry land. Strong and mentally tough, they will swim long distances, fight swift current, and bull through dense vegetation to find downed game. Extra body fat and thick double coats (a water-repellent outer coat overlaying a tight, insulating inner coat) protect them from cold and wet. On land they are expected to walk at heel, stand or sit quietly, and fetch after the shooting is done. In addition, most retrievers can be taught to work like spaniels, probing into upland cover to flush game for the gun.

Because their tasks require them to cooperate closely with humans, retrievers have been bred to be easy to train and control. They can be taught to make "blind" retrieves, following whistle and arm signals to find a bird they didn't see fall—an impressive feat of teamwork that often saves game otherwise lost. Yet simple obedience training, combined with the retriever's natural desire to please and its strong propensity to fetch, is often all that is needed to develop an effective hunting dog.

One of the nicest things about a retriever is the close bond it develops with its master. Except when working, the dog sits beside the hunter, so there is plenty of opportunity for petting, ear-scratching, nuzzling, and rubbing shoulders. Retrievers just naturally love humans—and, just as naturally, we respond.

The Labrador retriever is the most popular retrieving breed— in fact, the most popular hunting dog in America today. The Chesapeake Bay retriever is the biggest and toughest retriever, capable of plowing through icy water and heavy seas and handling big fowl like Canada geese. The golden retriever is handsome, personable, intelligent, and effective in the uplands. The flat-coated and curly-coated retrievers are uncommon but useful breeds whose rarity or appearance may be just what a certain hunter is looking for. The Irish water spaniel—the only spaniel classed with the retrievers—is a large, strong dog capable of hauling in geese. The Nova Scotia duck tolling retriever is named for its ability to attract or "toll in" curious waterfowl by running and frisking along the shore. Except for the Nova Scotia duck tolling retriever, all retrievers—whether from hunting or show stock—are registered with the American Kennel Club.

Retrievers peaked in popularity on the American hunting scene during the 1800s, when waterfowl were richly abundant. Until 1900, there were no bag limits on ducks and geese: Gunners —including market hunters—might take scores of fowl each day, day after day. They needed, and vigorously used, hard-working retrievers. When duck populations dwindled and fledgling conservation agencies began setting seasons and bag limits, a spendthrift era came to an end, the market hunter vanished, and the use of retrievers fell off. More hunters began using pointing dogs in the uplands, drawing their pleasure from stylish dog work rather than from gargantuan bags of game.

The last thirty to forty years have seen retrievers steadily gain in popularity as flush-hunters of upland birds. The average retriever —trainable, obedient, of moderate speed afoot—does a good job for the hunter who lacks the time or inclination to conduct the extensive training needed to polish a pointing dog. A retriever is the correct choice for the hunter who concentrates on waterfowl, but who also hunts upland birds and prefers the game to be flushed rather than pointed. If the hunter specializes in upland game and only occasionally pursues waterfowl, one of the flushing spaniels is a better choice, since it will tend to cover the ground more efficiently.

Because of their genial, cooperative natures, most retrievers make fine indoor dogs, although they can be too big or unruly for some households. Most are also good watchdogs, raising the alarm when strangers approach.

Resources

Water Dog, Richard A. Wolters. Dutton, New York, 1964.

Gun-Dog Training: Spaniels and Retrievers, Kenneth C. Roebuck. Stackpole, Harrisburg, PA, 1982.

Hunting Retrievers: Hindsights, Foresights, Insights, James B. Spencer. Alpine Publications, Loveland, CO, 1989.

"The Hunting Retriever Movement," Jerome B. Robinson. *Sports Afield*, August 1986.

"Retrieve" column, James B. Spencer. *Gun Dog* (bimonthly), Stover Publishing, P.O. Box 35098, Des Moines, IA 50315.

Labrador
RETRIEVER

T he market hunter picked his way through the straggling, chest-high birch and willow. He was a tall, lean Icelander with cleated boots, snow gaiters, a leather strap for his birds, and a scarred Browning over-and-under. His gangly yellow Labrador, all of five months old, heeled beside her master across the snow-covered slope.

I stopped my own hunting to watch them. He moved steadily through the thicket, and she with him, falling back where the shintangle pinched in, resuming at his side where the growth allowed it. Two birds went out. White as the snow, the ptarmigan flashed away above the reddish brown scrub; one had already fallen and the second was collapsing in a puff of feathers when the Browning's first report reached my ears.

He sent her for the first bird and accepted the retrieve; with a quick hand signal he released her for the second. She extracted it from the depths of a patch of creeping willow and brought it back, her tail wagging proudly. The young Lab still had her milk

An excellent all-purpose breed, the Labrador retriever is the most popular hunting dog today.

teeth. Already she had fetched two hundred ptarmigan since the season opened two weeks earlier, and, over the next two months, no doubt she would retrieve hundreds more.

That kind of performance at such a young age would be too much to ask of many breeds, but not of a Labrador retriever. The Labrador is probably the most popular gun dog in the world today, and for good reason. It learns quickly. It can fetch from land or water. It can be taught to work before the gun, flushing and then retrieving game. The Labrador's calm, cooperative nature makes it a fine companion; it is sociable with other dogs and hunters.

The Labrador is strong and solidly built, has short ears and a thick otterlike tail, and, overall, projects a no-frills, utilitarian aspect. Males weigh sixty to seventy-five pounds and stand twenty-two to twenty-four inches at the shoulder; bitches weigh fifty-five to seventy pounds and are an inch or two shorter.

One of the Labrador's excellent characteristics is a short, dense, watertight coat that cleans easily and does not pick up burs and sticktights. The dog is not hampered by a buildup of water, ice, or mud; it does not leave a mess on the inside of a blind or a vehicle, nor does the hunter have to spend an hour grooming the dog after a long day in the field. This low-maintenance wrapper comes in three colors: black (the majority of Labs are black), chocolate (a rich dark brown), and yellow (ranging from a pale creamy color to a reddish foxlike hue).

Black is the genetically dominant color; chocolate and yellow are recessive. Selective breeding for a yellow or a chocolate litter requires breeding yellow and chocolate dogs and may produce pups with less potential hunting ability: After all, nose, biddability, intelligence, and hunting desire were not the primary traits for which the match was made. It is the black Labrador that dominates the field trial scene and, on average, makes the more trainable companion and better hunter. However, mating two excellent Labs (even two black dogs) may still yield yellow or chocolate puppies. Hunting dog authority Dave Duffey writes: "I wouldn't hesitate to buy, or take in for training, a yellow or chocolate [Labrador] that had black littermates. But I'd be pretty skeptical about a pup from an all yellow, all chocolate, or mixed yellow and chocolate litter."

The Labrador retriever does not come from Labrador, at least not precisely. It is an English breed. The most recent scholarship, by the writer and dog training expert Richard Wolters, suggests that it derives from St. Hubert's hound, a French dog brought to England in the 1500s. Fishermen from Devon, in western England, took their St. Hubert's hounds with them to Newfoundland, an island off the coast of Labrador. There the dogs were used both for hunting and to retrieve fish that would thrash off the hook when a long line was brought up from the ocean. Three centuries later, sea captains returned the breed to England; by then it was called the St. John's dog, after the settlement in Newfoundland.

The Labrador retriever as we know it was developed in the 1800s by the aristocracy in England and Scotland. The dogs were used mainly on shoots sponsored by the owners of large private estates. They would sit with their handlers while guests shot pheasants or grouse driven past by beaters; when the smoke cleared, the dogs would fetch.

In the 1920s, America's moneyed aristocracy got a taste of this "driven bird shooting," and liked it. In true Yankee fashion, they imported the British tradition—gamekeepers, trainers, dogs, and all. At that time, two homegrown breeds dominated the retrieving scene: the American water spaniel and the Chesapeake Bay retriever. Before long, Labs owned by people with names like Remick and Harriman and Carlisle and Guggenheim were sweeping the retriever field trials. It took a while for the Lab to trickle down to less-well-heeled hunters, but as the breed's strong points and versatility became known, it supplanted the Chesapeake and American water spaniel as America's premier retriever. Wolters estimates there are 1.8 million hunting Labs in the United States today.

The Labrador bridges the gap between today's two other popular retrievers, the Chesapeake and golden. The Chesapeake is bigger, tougher, more rugged: If the game is geese and the weather brutal, the Chesapeake will excel. The average Chesapeake is more independent than the Lab, less lovable (sometimes to the point of irascibility), and often aggressive toward other dogs and humans. The handsome, affable golden stands at the opposite end of the spectrum: A "soft" dog, it responds best to praise, coaxing, and repetition in training. When the going gets tough, the golden will flag before the Chesapeake or Lab will. The Labrador is a more versatile dog than either of these other breeds. It is generally more available, and an excellent bet for the home trainer. Overzealous training and a beginner's mistakes rarely ruin a Lab.

The prospective Labrador owner must buy from proven field trial or hunting stock, rather than from show stock or from someone who simply "has Labs" and breeds them for fun or to sell puppies. In the retrievers, field trial lines have been developed to produce trainable, avid bird finders: precisely the qualities that make for good hunters. (Although complaints are beginning to be heard about Labs being too intense or high-strung, keyed up for trial work and "more dog" than the average hunter wants to train or handle.) Two possible strategies are to buy from another hunter whose dogs you have seen in action, or to find a litter produced by dogs that have excelled in hunting retriever tests. These tests, conducted under actual field conditions, evaluate marking, retrieving, tracking, and quartering skills. Dogs are judged against a written standard and win points toward various rankings.

At one time, Labradors were used almost exclusively to fetch ducks and geese. When duck populations and duck-hunting opportunities plummeted in the 1960s and 1970s, Labradors stayed popular, thanks to their prowess at hunting upland birds. With a modest amount of training, the field-bred Labrador will do a creditable job on any game the hunter wants to pursue: doves, pheasants, woodcock, ruffed grouse, Hungarian partridge, sharp-tailed grouse, prairie chickens, sage grouse, bobwhite quail, jacksnipe, and rails. Dave Duffey, who has owned and trained many Labs, writes: "Probably seventy-five to eighty percent of the Labs out of hunting and field trial stock will become adept [at] producing upland birds for the gun, particularly pheasants. Most will learn to hunt in the manner of a spaniel, quartering after a fashion and probing cover clumps within gun range to flush birds that would otherwise have sat tight or sneaked off. Even the small percentage who don't display much natural 'hunt,' if trained as nonslip retrievers and kept under strict control, may be walked at heel, from whence they can be sent to pick up shot birds or cast into a likely clump to roust out a skulker on pheasant drives."

The Labrador makes a good house pet and watchdog. It is sometimes a bit too robust and rough for small children, and its thick tail, wagged in the wrong place, can clean off a coffee table. Not only a hunter, the Lab works at herding stock, detecting drugs, and guiding the blind. If any sporting breed comes close to being an all-around dog, it is the Labrador retriever.

Summary: Medium to large, exceptionally popular hunting breed used to retrieve ducks and geese and flush a range of upland birds. Good dove dog. Mild, biddable; can often be hunted when less than a year old. Coat requires almost no care. Widely available in hunting and field trial bloodlines: Be careful to avoid pet and show stock.

Resources

The Labrador Retriever: The History . . . The People, Richard A. Wolters. Petersen Prints, Los Angeles, 1981.

"The Lab: Versatile Virtuoso," Dave Duffey. *Gun Dog,* February/March 1990.

"Labs: Everyman's Gundog," Jerome B. Robinson. *Sports Afield,* November 1989.

Big, strong, and tough-minded, the Chesapeake Bay retriever can handle frigid water and wounded game better than any other breed.

Chesapeake Bay
RETRIEVER

A punt gun was a daunting firearm, a shotgun inches across the muzzle, up to twelve feet long, and mounted in a low, flat-bottomed boat. It was a favorite tool of the market hunter on the Atlantic seaboard who, in the era before hunting seasons and bag limits, made his living killing ducks and geese for the urban market. Wrote one nineteenth-century observer: "Every hour during the night can be heard the sullen boom of these swivels floating across the waters, and the true sportsman, as he listens to the echoing roar, can only grind his teeth with rage, for he knows what a slaughter is going on."

The market hunter needed a tireless, tough dog to fetch the scores of dead and crippled waterfowl, often at night and in horrendous weather. Too, he needed a possessive, scrappy canine that would guard his decoys, gear, and the daily take. He found such a dog in the Chesapeake Bay retriever.

The Chesapeake is one of four sporting breeds developed on the North American continent. (The others are the American

water spaniel, the Boykin spaniel, and the Nova Scotia duck tolling retriever.) The Chesapeake's story begins in 1807, when an
English brig carrying codfish stopped at a Chesapeake Bay port
for a load of wood, then departed for Poole Harbor, England.
Soon after, the ship sank in a gale, and an American vessel rescued the crew, along with two water dog puppies—a male "of a
dingy red color" and a black female. These dogs were of a type
called the St. John's dog, which, over the next seventy years, the
English would refine and develop into the Labrador retriever; on
the rough-and-tumble shores of the Chesapeake—springing from
those two shipwrecked canines—the St. John's dog would become the more formidable Chesapeake Bay retriever.

In 1845, George Law, the Marylander who had saved the shipwrecked dogs and later sold them to acquaintances, wrote: "Both
attained great reputations as water dogs. They were most saga-
cious in everything, particularly in all duties connected with duck
shooting." The bitch, named Canton, "remained at Sparrows Point
[on the western shore of Maryland] till her death, and her prog-
eny were and still are well known through Patapsco Neck, on the
Gunpowder, and up the bay." The male, Sailor, ended up on the
Eastern Shore, where his offspring inherited, in addition to his
hunting abilities, his peculiar eye coloring, "so light as to have an
almost unnatural appearance."

Although Sailor and Canton were never bred to each other,
they were paired with other excellent dogs. Over the generations,
pointers, setters, flat-coated retrievers, Irish water spaniels, and
black-and-tan hounds are thought to have added to the Chesapeake. The breed even received an influx of otter genes (or so the
story goes) when a bitch in heat was tied to a tree and left
overnight near an otter's den. The Chesapeake was bred for
courage, size, strength, and endurance. In the harsh environment
in which the breed evolved, the poor worker was swiftly dis-
carded, the unsound and weak broke down under the relentless
work, and the strong and the tough survived.

Wealthy sportsmen, it is believed, later developed selective breeding programs that stabilized the breed. During its development, the Chesapeake acquired several names: Chesapeake Bay duck dog, Gunpowder River dog, otter dog, and the "brown Winchester," which, according to *The American Sportsman,* "does not shiver like a setter, or raise and drop his forefeet like a wet spaniel; the shaking he has given his wet, oily coat, has freed it entirely from ice and water."

As the Chesapeake's reputation grew, it began to be used throughout the United States. A rigorous selectivity continued. From the brochure of Jay F. Towner, Locust Grove, Maryland, who bred Chesapeakes from 1860 to 1904: "I guarantee every pup to make a good retriever if properly trained, or party can kill him, send me the certificate of his death, and I will send another pup free." Another breeder bragged of his stud dog: "Never lost a fight or a duck."

The Chesapeake of today remains a big, strong, self-contained dog that looks as tough as a canine can get. The average Chessie weighs a burly sixty-five to seventy pounds (although big males can exceed eighty) and stands up to twenty-six inches at the shoulder. The Chesapeake has extra-long hind legs to propel it through the water; thus the hips are a shade higher than the shoulders and the back is a bit swayed. Heavily webbed toes and a thick rudder of a tail aid the dog in swimming.

The breed shows much variety in coloring: tan, a bright light red, a deep reddish chestnut, flat brown, chocolate, and a light straw color, termed "deadgrass," developed in the Midwest. A small amount of white is acceptable on breast, belly, or toes. The eyes are yellow.

More important than the coat's color are its functional aspects. The outer fur is thick, harsh, and relatively short, not over one and a half inches, wavy except on the legs and face, oily to repel water. The undercoat is soft, woolly, and insulating.

The Chesapeake is the dog for the hard-core waterfowler. It

can hunt day after day, shrugging off the cold and the wet, retrieving repeatedly under conditions that would literally kill other dogs. It can break ice to retrieve a bird. It will enter bitterly cold water enthusiastically, including salt water, which does not freeze until it reaches 27 degrees Fahrenheit. The Chessie is the goose dog of choice, able to retrieve wounded birds that would punish, or even drive off, a lesser dog. It will buck strong current, negotiate choppy seas, and dive after a wounded duck. It can learn to mark down a half-dozen birds at a time. It will selectively fetch cripples, then go back and finish up on the floating dead fowl. When all is said and done, the Chesapeake is the finest working water dog in the world.

The breed reached the zenith of its popularity by the end of the same century in which it arose. By the 1900s, market hunting had so decimated waterfowl populations that sport hunters turned more to upland game. Enter the Labrador and golden retrievers, which do a better job as dry-land flushing dogs. Today, Labs and goldens greatly outnumber Chesapeakes: in 1990, 95,768 Labs and 64,848 goldens were registered with the American Kennel Club (an unknown percentage of these were pets and show dogs), compared to 4,272 Chesapeakes.

Although less maneuverable on land than the other retrievers, the Chesapeake can be taught to work in front of the gun to put up birds for the hunter. It can be used as a nonslip retriever, heeling with the hunter until directed to fetch. It will retrieve doves.

The Chesapeake has the reputation of being a "one-man dog," better trained over long periods by its master than through short-term stays with a professional. The retriever authority James Spencer writes, "You train a golden; you distract a Labrador; you negotiate with a Chesapeake." A Chesapeake can be stubborn and hard to train, a "hands-on" sort of dog that responds best to an assertive, consistent owner willing to spend plenty of time at the task. Interestingly, some respected trainers insist that the

Chesapeake responds best to the coaxing one would normally use to train a golden, and "turns off" or ignores the handler when subjected to a more rigorous, tougher approach.

In recent years the Chesapeake has gotten a lot of bad press for being too aggressive, too protective of its owner and its owner's possessions, family, and home—a trait recalling the Chessie's beginnings as a market hunter's sometime-retriever, sometime-guard dog. From *The Complete Chesapeake Bay Retriever*, by Eloise Heller Cherry: "The efforts of today's fanciers to breed Chesapeakes which can fit into the average modern household—with a family of kids, next-door neighbors, numbers of strangers coming in the house as guests, delivery men, meter readers, postmen and others—have been entirely successful with some dogs, partially so with others, and not at all with still others." In general, Labrador and golden retrievers are more sociable than Chesapeakes, something to keep in mind considering today's litigious society. Chesapeakes are also prone to fighting with other dogs. The breed benefits from early socialization, contact with people and other canines during the formative period from seven to twelve weeks of age.

Because of its bulk, temperament, and utilitarian appearance, the Chesapeake has never been overly popular as a pet or show dog. Writes Cherry, "Good hunting dogs really are the backbone of our breed." The classified section of a recent issue of *Gun Dog* magazine had advertisements from breeders in North Carolina, Minnesota, Tennessee, Arkansas, Idaho, Illinois, New Jersey, and Kansas—surprisingly, none from Maryland, where this hardy, tough-minded water dog arose.

Summary: Large, strong, aggressive. Top choice for dedicated waterfowler: Handles geese and frigid conditions best of all breeds. Can be trained to hunt upland birds, though Labrador and golden retrievers do a better job. Some Chesapeakes are surly and may turn on other dogs and people. May be too big to live in a smaller house.

Resources

The Complete Chesapeake Bay Retriever, Eloise H. Cherry. Howell Book House, New York, 1981.

The Chesapeake Bay Retriever, Arthur S. Beaman. Denlinger, Fairfax, VA, 1981.

"The Chesapeake Bay Retriever," Emelise Baughman. *Gun Dog*, March/April 1984.

Golden RETRIEVER

O f all the retrievers, the golden is the most affectionate. It wears a beautiful, soft coat of a warm golden hue, and its face is often set in an expression of intelligent affability. The golden is a popular dog; in 1990 the American Kennel Club registered almost 65,000 goldens, ranking the breed fourth in overall popularity, behind the cocker spaniel, Labrador retriever, and poodle.

An interesting apocryphal story about the golden's origin was treated as gospel for many years: In 1860 Sir Dudley Marjoribanks, the Lord Tweedmouth (so named because his estate lay at the mouth of the Tweed River in southwestern Scotland), was so impressed by some Russian circus dogs performing at Brighton, England, that he bought the entire troupe of eight. The dogs, called "Russian trackers," were bred by Lord Tweedmouth into a line of golden-furred retrievers. Lord Tweedmouth was in fact the originator of the golden retriever, but he developed the breed in a rather more prosaic manner, by crossing a rare blond flat-coated

The handsome, affable golden retriever is a good choice for a mix of upland hunting and waterfowl retrieving.

retriever (then called a wavy-coated retriever) with a breed now extinct, the Tweed water spaniel.

Originally considered simply a color phase of the flat-coat, the golden was granted separate status by the English Kennel Club in 1913. The American Kennel Club recognized the breed in 1932, when the retrieving scene in the United States was dominated by Chesapeake Bay and Labrador retrievers. Popularity of the golden rose gradually through the forties and fifties; in the 1970s President Gerald Ford brought one into the White House, and soon Madison Avenue had goldens cavorting in ads for everything from whiskey to station wagons: Suddenly the breed was all the rage.

Today most goldens are produced for the pet market (as are most Labradors), with no care given to preserving hunting instincts, so it can be hard to find one with an honest hunting heritage. A current authority on the breed asserts that there are now two types, field and bench—however, "the bench-bred goldens have retained their working ability." Other authorities would disagree and label the bench golden as "worthless." The hunter wishing to maximize the odds of getting a solid hunting golden should be extremely selective and choose puppies only from parents who hunt.

The current breed standard calls for males to be twenty-three to twenty-four inches at the withers and to weigh sixty-five to seventy-five pounds; bitches should be twenty-one and a half to twenty-two and a half inches tall and weigh fifty-five to sixty-five pounds. This is about the same size as a Labrador retriever. The golden is an active, strong-looking dog, not clumsy or overly long-legged, built to get around with agility on land and in the water.

The golden is an all-around hunter. The least water-loving of the retriever breeds, it is not as rugged as a Labrador or a Chesapeake: If you are a waterfowl specialist accustomed to hunting in brutal weather and need a canine to brave icy water to make retrieve after retrieve, then the golden is not your dog. If, on the other hand, you go out after ducks a good bit, also hunt pheasants, sometimes venture into grouse and woodcock thickets, and post along the edges of cornfields for doves in early fall—then a golden will do a good job. Like the English springer spaniel, it is very much a dog for "rough-shooting," the English term describing a hunt when several kinds of game may be taken in varied terrain, the sort of hunting that most Americans do.

Depending on how you view it, the golden's coat is a great asset or a distinct disadvantage. The fur is a feast for the eyes, thick and luxuriant, the color of a stubblefield bathed in January light. But after you follow a golden through a typical pheasant covert, you may face an hour of combing and plucking out burs and sticktights. On a duck hunt, the coat soaks up water that has to drip off somewhere—on the floor of the blind, in the boat, in the car after the hunt.

The golden has an excellent nose, which most experts rate a bit keener than the Labrador's. A seasoned golden will follow cripples for long distances and retrieve many birds that otherwise would be lost. The breed has an exceptionally soft mouth and will fetch capably from land, marsh, or open water. The breed's temperament is probably its best point: loving, cheerful, alert, eagerly cooperative. The golden is the most spaniel-like of the retrieving breeds in its biddability and desire to please.

Goldens tend to be "soft" dogs, responding to praise, reassurance, and positive reinforcement during training. A person inclined toward strict or rough training methods should not choose a golden. As one trainer writes, "[Goldens] respond so well to positive training techniques that there is seldom any excuse for being rough with them." Because a golden matures less quickly than a Labrador, you will be able to enjoy serious hunting with a Lab well before a golden will be ready. But although the breed develops slowly, it tends to remember its lessons longer and requires less retraining every year. The golden readily learns whistle and hand signals, and can carry out difficult tasks like blind retrieves. The breed dominates American Kennel Club obedience trials, and is widely used as a guide dog for the blind. An excellent choice for the amateur trainer, it requires a minimum of schooling to become an acceptable hunter.

The golden is dedicated to its master and family, and its friendly, open demeanor extends to other canines and to humans outside the family circle. Goldens are great with children and do not represent a menace to mail carriers, meter readers, and other household visitors: Watchdogs they are not. About the only negative aspect of having a golden in the house is, again, that lovely long coat, which, if not combed regularly, sheds onto floor, carpet, pant legs, and furniture.

Theodore A. Rehm, in 1948 in *American Sporting Dogs*, gives a synopsis of the golden retriever that rings true to this day: "A field dog of unsurpassed performance, plus outstanding beauty of appearance, plus a temperament that makes one's hunting dog a perfect house companion for the months out of the year when there is no gunning." Yet the golden was then, and still is, second choice to the Labrador as America's premier hunting retriever. Why? The Lab is tougher and more efficiently trained: It wins all the field trials and so gets all the fame. Its manner, while not as winning as the golden's, is upbeat, intelligent, and friendly. And— perhaps the key—the Labrador's coat requires much less care.

Summary: Medium to large, excels on upland birds, will retrieve from land and water. A good first dog. Slow to mature but extremely intelligent, a joy to train; requires a light hand in training. Loving to owner, friendly to other humans and dogs. Coat requires frequent, ongoing maintenance. Fairly high incidence of canine hip dysplasia (CHD).

Resources

The Complete Golden Retriever, Gertrude Fischer. Howell Book House, New York, 1974.

"The Golden Retriever," James B. Spencer. *Gun Dog,* July/August 1984.

The Golden Retriever News (see "Field" section), Julie Cairns, 131 River View Lane, Arcata, CA 95521.

Flat-Coated
RETRIEVER

F or many years the flat-coated retriever was the favorite of gamekeepers on British estates. The keepers were often directed by their employers to harvest game for the manor table; they needed a close-working, keen-nosed retriever, kept under the strictest control, that could be hunted on the fringes of the game-producing estate, leaving the main habitat for the owner's sport and never blundering onto adjacent properties. The dog was expected to flush game, work any sort of cover, find wounded birds, and retrieve from land and water. At these basic hunting tasks, the flat-coated retriever excelled.

Today—despite a handsome appearance, a strong working background, and a hunting ardor that has never waned—the flat-coat is rare in England and even rarer in the United States. In 1990 the American Kennel Club registered 442 flat-coats in eighty-seven litters, placing it far behind the Labrador (95,768 dogs), golden (64,848), and Chesapeake Bay retrievers (4,272).

The flat-coat came into existence in England in the 1800s,

Known as "the gamekeeper's dog" in Britain, the flat-coated retriever is a rare breed both in England and the United States.

when St. John's dogs (also the foundation stock for the Labrador and Chesapeake) were crossed with water spaniels, Irish setters, and perhaps Gordon setters; the setter crosses are said to have given the flat-coat its excellent sense of smell. The first flat-coat to gain public recognition appeared in a dog show in 1860. Dr. Bond Moore of Wolverhampton is credited as the major developer of the breed, then called the "wavy-coated retriever." The flat-coat achieved popularity as a field trial performer, but soon lost out to the faster, more efficiently trained Labrador. No doubt it is the Labrador's ongoing success in the field trial world that has relegated the flat-coat to obscurity over the last seventy years—even though the flat-coat has the potential to be a superb gun dog and hunting companion in its own right.

The flat-coated retriever stands twenty-four inches and weighs sixty to seventy pounds, a bit taller and lankier than the Labrador. The traditional color is jet black, although some individuals are liver (similar to the chocolate color in the Labrador). The coat is longer and softer than the Lab's, shorter and less abundant than the golden's. The flat-coat's fur is weather-resistant and protects against thorns; it does not attract burs and sticktights too readily.

Flat-coats cover the ground with a fluid, graceful gait. From the breed standard, adopted in 1923 and still current: "The flat-coated retriever combines substance and strength with elegance and refinement; which together with a happy and active demeanor, intelligent expression, and clean lines, have been eloquently described as *power without lumber and raciness without weediness.*" The head is rather long, without an exaggerated "stop" (the up-slant of the skull behind the nose and in front of the eyes), the jaws long and strong, able to carry large game like hares, ducks, and pheasants.

There is no split between show and field flat-coats. Today, the major emphasis within the breed is on the show ring, yet the field qualities of the flat-coat are said to be as strong as ever, and many are excelling in licensed hunting tests. The Flat-Coated Retriever Society of America sponsors a Working Certificate (WC) program that encourages owners to train their dogs in the basics of hunting and fetching. The modern flat-coat is described in the society's brochure as "a resourceful, birdy gamefinder and a determined, soft-mouthed retriever . . . a bright, enthusiastic, durable dog, whose character and temperament are well suited to being a responsive, versatile, and devoted companion."

The key word is "companion." In a recent article, longtime breeder Nancy Kerns, of McHenry, Illinois, is quoted as saying, "The flat-coated retriever was developed as a personal hunting dog. They are companions, very people-oriented, and require close interaction with their master or family at all times."

According to its supporters, the flat-coat is the epitome of the canine extrovert, with boundless enthusiasm, an endlessly wagging tail, and a sunny disposition. Says Kerns, "Flat-coats are intelligent and quick to learn. But they can't be repeatedly drilled on the same routine, and they don't take well to mechanical training methods." Like the golden retriever, the flat-coat responds to positive training techniques and plenty of praise. Some flat-coats can be slow developers, requiring great patience as they mature. The breed is long-lived; says Kerns, "They are usually as active and strong at ten or twelve years as they were when they were pups."

Prentice Talmage, an authority on the flat-coat, wrote in the 1948 compendium *American Sporting Dogs:* "Hunting seasons are very short, and you have to live with your dog for the rest of the year. The flat-coated retriever makes an ideal, quiet, affectionate and clean dog in the house. He is obedient, well mannered and devoted to his master and his family. I know of no better dog with children." Wrote William Brown, in his 1945 classic *Retriever Gun Dogs*, "Whether for water work or upland game shooting, the flat-coat is adept at marking, a superior retriever, and possessed of superb style." Across half a century, the words of both these experts still ring true.

The biggest problem connected with owning a flat-coated retriever is simply finding a litter from which to get a pup. The good news is that since flat-coats have remained relatively unknown, the breed has never suffered from a loss of quality and type caused by overbreeding to meet popular demand—increasingly a problem with the Labrador and golden. If you can locate a flat-coat, it will probably have a high potential as a gun dog—a very personal sort of hunting companion.

Summary: Medium to large, lanky, all-purpose retriever for land and water, especially good in uplands. Coat resists weather and thorns, requires moderate upkeep. Good-natured, obedient, long-lived. No split between show and hunting lines. Rare.

Resources

The Complete Flat-Coated Retriever, Paddy Petch. Howell Book House, New York, 1988.

A Review of the Flat-Coated Retriever, Nancy Laughton. Pelham Books, London, 1980.

"Flat-Coats: The Unsung Retrievers," Rick Van Etten. *Gun Dog*, January/February 1986.

Flat-Coated Retriever Society of America: Valerie Bernhardt, R.R. 2, Box 9300A, Milford, PA 18337.

The powerful, rugged curly-coated retriever is independent and slow to mature.

Curly-Coated RETRIEVER

A popular 1960s book on hunting dogs virtually dismissed the curly-coated retriever, citing a coat that "picks up burs and all sorts of twigs and grasses beyond belief."

Not so, claim a small but growing number of men and women who hunt with this sturdy breed. They say the curly-coated retriever's fur—short, hard-textured, curly almost to the point of kinkiness—is actually a low-maintenance cloak. Burs and stick-tights cling to the springy surface but fail to penetrate. Writes Janean Marti of Cadott, Wisconsin, "As a lazy dog owner, I find the coat ideal. Normally, by the time we arrive home [after a hunt], the dogs have picked any burs or seeds out of their coats and carefully deposited them on the pickup floor. It is a simple matter to pluck any seeds they miss."

The widespread prejudice against its coat has probably held back this traditional hunting breed. Only around a thousand curly-coated retrievers exist in the United States, producing roughly one hundred pups in twenty to twenty-five litters annually. And the curly, as its loyalists call it, is scarcely more popular in England, where the breed arose.

In 1860 the English sporting author Stonehenge wrote of the curly, "This variety of retriever is always a cross between the St. John's [dog] and the water spaniel, which is generally Irish." Actually, the curly's origins are more obscure than that, with various early retrieving strains combining with the basic St. John's stock; possibly the old German poodle contributed the curly coat. Like the related flat-coated retriever, the close-working curly was a favorite of nineteenth-century English gamekeepers.

Today's curly-coated retriever is a powerful, rugged dog suitable for retrieving ducks and geese in frigid water, and a respectable hunter in the uplands. Interestingly, the breed standard published by the Curly-Coated Retriever Club of America not only does not specify size, it actually emphasizes that there are no restrictions on height or weight. Midwestern pheasant hunters, facing thick bottomland coverts, may want their curlys small: twenty-one inches and fifty pounds. North Atlantic waterfowlers may prefer bigger dogs, up to thirty inches and one hundred pounds. Most curlys fall between these extremes. The breed tends to be deep-chested and long-legged, with a wiry rather than a burly build.

Back to that unique coat. The texture has been compared to that of astrakhan wool. The tight curls extend from the back of the head down over the elbows and hocks, back over the body to the tip of the straight, saber-shape tail. The hair on the face and the lower legs is smooth and straight. Color is overall black or liver.

According to retriever authority James B. Spencer, "In water the curly is far better protected than the golden and flat-coat, significantly better protected than the Irish water spaniel and Labrador, and about equally as well protected as the Chesapeake." The close curls supposedly keep the dog's skin from getting wet and cold. A curly can retrieve a goose from an ice-filled bay, shake itself dry, sit back down without a shiver, and patiently wait for the next fetch.

Spencer continues: "No other retriever breed's coat is as briar- and bramble-proof as the curly's. That tight, hard mass of curls will withstand any cover." Where a Labrador may skirt a patch of thorns, a curly will plunge right in. And—all prejudices aside— its fur won't snarl with burs as a golden's will.

As unique as its coat is this retriever's temperament. The curly is not as ebullient as the golden. It is not as aggressively coopera- tive as the Labrador. Nor is it as tough-minded as the Chesa- peake. Its proponents agree that the curly-coated retriever is intelligent, that it is far happier and better-adjusted as a house dog than in a kennel, and that it is deeply affectionate toward its master and family. It is reserved toward strange humans, but will tolerate them. Its devotion and protectiveness make it a good watchdog.

Curlys are the slowest of the retriever breeds to leave puppy- hood behind. Few will be physically or mentally mature by age two, and many will take until age four to really grow up. When it gets ready to learn, though, a curly-coated retriever will put things together quickly and remember its lessons well. The breed was developed to hunt and retrieve following a minimum of train- ing; with some dogs, instilling a basic obedience is all that is necessary. Writes Spencer, "If you use a curly like the game- keepers always have, relying more on the dog's instincts than on formal training, you will be delighted with [its] performance most of the time." Compared to some other retriever breeds, curlys are less able (or less inclined) to learn complicated tasks such as taking a line or making a blind retrieve. The curly-coated re- triever's greatest assets are its natural hunting instinct, drive, and perseverence.

In the uplands a curly soon learns to quarter through likely looking habitat. The breed can be used on a range of upland gamebirds. Not as fast or as stylish as a Labrador or a golden, a curly will hunt at a steady, tireless pace, and because it works slowly, it will usually flush its birds within gun range. Some curlys hesitate before flushing in a sort of rudimentary point.

One reads about curlys amusing themselves by swimming around for hours on end, or diving and bringing up rocks and logs from the bottoms of ponds: Clearly, the breed loves the water. Curlys learn quickly from experience, figuring out how to negotiate river currents and thick streamside cover. Natural, soft-mouthed retrievers, they are capable of handling all waterfowl. They will dive repeatedly to catch crippled ducks, and they mark downed game capably. In Australia and New Zealand, where the breed is fairly popular, curlys retrieve swans weighing twenty-five pounds.

Probably most curlys in the United States are hunting dogs. Because they are so few, litters are often sold in advance, and there can be a long waiting list for dogs from excellent stock. Susan Tokolics of West Chester, Pennsylvania, shows as well as hunts her dogs. She estimates that seventy-five percent of curlys have the potential to become acceptable hunters.

Summary: Medium to large, powerful, rugged, good for retrieving waterfowl in bad weather or birds in uplands. Coat resists thorns, burs. Matures slowly, then trains quickly. Devoted, protective, good watchdog. Rare.

Resources

"The Curly-Coated Retriever," Janean Marti. *Gun Dog*, January/February 1988.

"The Curly-Coated Retriever," James B. Spencer. *Wildfowl Magazine*, February/March 1987.

Curly-Coated Retriever Club of America: Gina Columbo, 24 Holmes Blvd., Fort Walton Beach, FL 32548.

The Irish water spaniel—the only spaniel to work primarily as a retriever—is often clownish, but devoted to owner and family.

Irish Water
SPANIEL

For a thumbnail sketch of this unique and individualistic breed, go no further than the title of a book about the Irish water spaniel: *A Bundle of Rags in a Cyclone.*

The dog's name is self-explanatory: A spaniel developed in Ireland for water work. The breed has been grouped with the retrievers because it is large, like the retrievers; because it works as a retriever, fetching ducks, geese, and upland game; and because when entered in field trials (something rarely done these days) it competes with the retrievers.

Water spaniels are referred to in Irish laws of A.D. 17 but whether those dogs are the antecedents of the modern Irish water spaniel is not known. Before 1850, two strains of water spaniels existed in Ireland, one in the north and one in the south. The northern strain were piebald and of medium size; the southern, used to hunt the bogs of the River Shannon, were large, dark, and curly-coated. From the southern stock, around the middle of the nineteenth century, a Dublin sportsman named Justin McCarthy refined the breed we know today.

Little is known of the specific animals used by McCarthy, who seems to have been a secretive man. A book published in 1847 cites his spaniels as "of the highest possible blood, and at the same time little inferior to Mastiffs in size and strength." McCarthy himself implied that he had added bloodhound genes to the mix. Poodles are a likely component, to reinforce intelligence, strong retrieving instincts, and a spectacularly curly coat. Other possible contributors are the St. John's dog and the curly-coated retriever.

It did not take long for the Irish water spaniel to reach America. Before 1860 the breed had become popular with waterfowlers along the Mississippi; it spread east and west from there. In 1884 in *The American Sportsman,* Elisha Lewis described the Irish water spaniel as "daily growing in favor." The breed's North American heyday came in the 1920s and 1930s. Since then it has dwindled, probably because other dogs have outshone it in field trials. Today there are around one thousand Irish water spaniels in the United States, with only ninety-four puppies and thirteen litters registered in 1990. The breed is primarily show-oriented: An estimated one in four Irishers is used as a hunting companion. Yet to compete in the show ring a dog must first earn a working certificate, indicating that owners intend to keep at least some of the breed's hunting instincts intact.

The Irish water spaniel is medium-size for a retrieving breed. Females stand about twenty-three inches at the shoulder and weigh sixty pounds; males are an inch taller and five pounds heavier. The chest is deep to provide plenty of lung capacity, and narrow so as not to hinder the limbs when the dog is swimming. Rear quarters are level with the shoulders or a trifle higher.

An Irish water spaniel's most distinctive feature is its dark brown coat (the color is sometimes described as puce). The coat features a woolly inner layer to hold warmth in cold weather and a curly outer layer to shed water and fend off thorns. The curls are dense, tight, crisp, and slightly oily. The retriever specialist James Spencer judges the Irish's coat more water-repellent than the golden retriever's, not quite as repellent as the Labrador's, and much less repellent than the Chesapeake's.

When an Irish water spaniel is worked exclusively in the water, its coat does not require excessive maintenance (although it will ice up in freezing weather). But when hunted in the uplands the dog will pick up burs and sticktights, which, if not promptly combed out, will render its fur a tangled mess. Nick Waters, the author of *A Bundle of Rags in a Cyclone*, writes: "If used . . . on a shoot with a lot of thick cover, a heavy coat may become more of a hindrance than anything else, and it does no harm to cut it short." Breed authority Elissa Kirkegard, of Doylestown, Pennsylvania, recommends that the coat be combed out and trimmed twice a year, once before hunting season and once during the spring shedding period.

The curly coat laps over onto the head in a distinctive dense topknot. The ears, which are long, are also cloaked with ringlets. The face is covered with naturally short hair, as is the tail (the Irish water spaniel is sometimes called the "rat-tail"). The coat does suggest a bundle of rags, and the dog's bouncy, frolicsome gait creates the impression of the cyclone whirling those rags around.

The Irish water spaniel lives up to its spaniel background in having a people-oriented, affectionate disposition. The breed is far happier in the house than in the kennel. Numerous observers have referred to the Irisher as a "one-family" as opposed to a "one-person" dog, meaning it will spread its love around freely within the human family with which it lives. It can be reserved with strangers and protective of its own turf.

A family member is the best person to train an Irish water spaniel. Although eager to please, the dog has a clownish nature that can get in the way of its education. Patience and firmness— never harshness—are necessary. One leads, encourages, and praises an Irish water spaniel. The Irisher is slow to mature, but, once trained, needs little brushing up in subsequent seasons. The breed's slow development and natural prankishness make it less than suitable for field trials, where precocity and instant obedience are rewarded.

The Irish water spaniel is notorious for its intelligence. Writes David Duffey in his training compendium, *Hunting Dog Know-How*, "Many members of this breed are just too smart for their own good. Not content to do just what a handler wants them to do, they'll try to find a different way to accomplish it, or throw in some sideline activity for good measure." The Irish water spaniel, Duffey concludes, is best appreciated by an owner "who possesses a sense of humor and a willingness to concede at times that his dog is smarter than he."

Thomas Marshall, of Southport, Connecticut, was a key breeder in the 1930s and a founder of the Irish Water Spaniel Club of America. He describes his dogs Bog and Jiggs in *American Sporting Dogs*, by Eugene Connett (1948), as "willing and intelligent workers who could think for themselves and this is true of most Irishers, that if they are taken gunning enough to get experience on wild birds, they will learn to do many things that you cannot teach them.

"Many a time I have been shooting from a duck boat in the marsh when the tide was high and Bog was returning with a downed blackduck, when another pair would start to lead into my stool. Bog would realize there were birds in the air, stop swimming and slide into a clump of sedge grass where he would remain motionless until I shot or called him in. And Jiggs soon learned to cut below the fall of a bird if the tide was running strong, and, if the tide was out and the bird came down with some life left in him, to hunt the guzzles and low spots where a blackduck would be likely to skulk."

Irish water spaniels are still as intelligent and water-loving today as they were half a century ago, although their hunting desire has been allowed to dwindle. Some Irishers can be trained to hunt like spaniels, quartering the ground to flush pheasant, woodcock, grouse, and other cover-dwelling birds. Some will retrieve doves. Historically the breed has done its best work in and along the water, following at the side of the jump-shooting hunter or sitting quietly in the blind until sent to fetch. A good Irisher will dive after wounded ducks, and have the strength and the courage to subdue crippled geese. The breed is widely credited with having an excellent nose and a soft retrieving mouth.

Summary: Medium to large, useful in uplands but more so in water. Retrieves all waterfowl, good on geese. Coat requires much maintenance. Friendly to owner and family, protective of home. Best taught by owner. Slow to mature, often prankish. Litters primarily from show stock; can be hard to find. Possesses less hunting desire than most other retriever breeds.

Resources

A Bundle of Rags in a Cyclone, Nick Waters. Benchworld Ltd., Crich, England, 1982.

"The Irish Water Spaniel," James B. Spencer. *Gun Dog*, September/October 1986.

The Irish Water Spaniel Club of America: Susan Tapp, 434 Webster Ave., Washington Township, NJ 07675.

Nova Scotia Duck Tolling
RETRIEVER

The verb "toll" comes from the Middle English *tollen*, to entice or lure. The Nova Scotia duck tolling retriever, or toller, was developed for the specific if improbable-sounding purpose of frolicking about on shore to entice waterfowl into shotgun range.

Tolling is in fact an ancient practice. Foxes do it: One of a pair plays along the water's edge; ducks spot the bright gamboling coat, grow curious, and paddle close to scold their ancient enemy —and the second fox pounces. Hundreds of years ago in Britain and Europe, hunters trained fox-colored dogs to toll ducks in to the net.

The exact origin of the Nova Scotia toller is obscure. European settlers—either French Acadians or Scots—brought the tradition with them. Or the settlers saw foxes tolling. Or they watched

An excellent marsh and upland dog, the Nova Scotia duck tolling retriever is gaining popularity in the United States.

Indians mimicking the vulpine technique, jiggling a fox fur on a string.

Regardless of who the settlers were or how they got the idea, they bred a dog that looked and acted like a fox. The Nova Scotia duck tolling retriever is a burnished red color, often with a white tail-tip, bouncy and animated in its movements. The breed is still used in Nova Scotia to toll in waterfowl. The technique is as follows:

The hunter builds a blind on the shore of a lake. When he sees ducks grouped, or "rafted," far out on the water, he hides in the blind and starts throwing a stick for his dog. The dog hustles out and fetches the stick, again and again. Sometimes the dog plays with the stick, tossing it into the air. The ducks notice the dog and start swimming toward it. (According to some sources, they may get so excited that they fly to the toller, or tumble over one another in their haste to approach.) The dog may retrieve the stick dozens of times, luring the ducks ever closer, while the fowl hiss and quack and slap the water with their wings. The dog in its sporting pays no attention to the ducks, which may approach within a few yards of the shore. Finally the hunter stands and shoots; then he sends the toller to fetch.

Mallards, teal, and scaup toll readily; Canada geese and black ducks, although among the wariest of waterfowl, are also vulnerable. Tolling has several advantages: It works on bright, sunny days, when most ducks will not respond to decoys or calling; it does not require a boat or decoys; and the hunter need not go out before dawn, since he must wait for the ducks to finish their morning feeding and raft up on open water to rest. Tolling is said not to work on small ponds, the moving waters of rivers, or where ducks are periodically disturbed by gunfire or passing boats.

Actually, even in Nova Scotia, where it is the most popular hunting dog, the toller is more often used as a standard hunting retriever than for actual tolling. Avery Nickerson, of Harbour

Light Kennels, Yarmouth, Nova Scotia, has bred tollers for fifty years and sold dogs to hunters in more than half of the United States and all of the Canadian provinces. As well as tolling ducks, his dogs are used to hunt grouse, woodcock, and pheasant. According to Nickerson, a toller will quarter and flush game more effectively than any other retriever and almost as well as a spaniel. Although tollers are excellent natural retrievers, for out-and-out fetching efficiency—especially on big birds like geese—Labradors and Chesapeakes rate higher.

A host of breeds have been nominated as contributors to the toller: flat-coated retriever, Labrador retriever, Chesapeake Bay retriever, cocker spaniel, Irish setter, Brittany, collie, and golden retriever. The toller was developed in the Little River district of southwestern Nova Scotia; until 1945, when the Canadian Kennel Club bestowed official recognition, the breed was known as the Little River duck dog. The Nova Scotia duck tolling retriever is not recognized by the American Kennel Club.

The toller is the smallest of the seven North American retriever breeds. The male stands about twenty inches at the shoulders and weighs around fifty pounds, with the female slightly smaller. The toller has a classic retriever's double coat: a long, straight, smooth outer coat to ward off water and thorns, over a thick, tight-knit, insulating inner coat. Short hair covers the face, legs, and ear tips. The toller's coat has a slightly coarser texture than a golden retriever's, so the Canadian breed can be expected to pick up fewer burs and sticktights.

Muscular and powerful, tollers move with a distinctive rushing action, the head carried out almost level with the back, the tail perpetually in motion. The breed is hardy, willing to plunge into icy water to make a retrieve. The retrieving instinct is deep-seated. When tolling in ducks, a dog may have to fetch a stick a hundred times: Other retrievers would soon get bored with such repetition, but the toller considers it fun. Nova Scotians refer to working a toller as "playing" the dog.

Tollers are docile, extremely intelligent, and devoted to their owners. They do not roam. They are gentle with children and get along well with other dogs. Suspicious of strangers, they make excellent watchdogs. Writes James Spencer in *Hunting Retrievers,* "Professional trainers frequently find the breed difficult to work with, while owners normally find them very easy. . . . The secret to training a toller lies in establishing and maintaining a rapport with the dog. Even the owner can bring out the animal's . . . stubbornness by being too heavy-handed, too sparing with praise and petting, or even by rushing things too much." The toller, concludes Spencer, "flourishes in an atmosphere of mutual respect, appreciation, and affection."

In Canada, some toller owners show their dogs in bench competition, but the breed has not lost its natural desire or ability to hunt. According to breeder Terry McNamee, "Almost any toller pup of eight or nine weeks old, chosen at random out of any litter, will immediately show a desire to retrieve any small object thrown for it." She describes the hunting toller as "intelligent, willing, able, and determined."

Summary: Medium size; smallest of retrievers. Lures in ducks or works as standard retriever or flusher. Good in cold water. Excels in uplands, although coat picks up burs. Docile, intelligent, good watchdog. Rare in United States.

Resources

"Decoy Dogs," Jerome B. Robinson. *Sports Afield,* August 1981.
"The Nova Scotia Duck Tolling Retriever," Colleen Archer. *Gun Dog,* January/February 1984.

"Canada's Unique Toller," Bill McClure. *Gun Dog*, November/ December 1986.

Canadian Kennel Club: 100-89 Skyway Ave., Etobicoke ONT, M9W 6R4, Canada.

III

POINTING DOGS

*You may hear him breaking
a twig, or splashing in a wet
spot, or plopping into the
creek. But when all sound
ceases, be ready for instant
action, for he is likely on
point.*

—Aldo Leopold
A Sand County Almanac

Among the spaniels, one occasionally finds a dog that will pause for a moment, catlike, before leaping in to flush. It is easy to imagine early hunters noticing this trait, and then breeding and training to strengthen it. The first pointing dogs "set" game so that hunters could throw a net over the birds (and often over the crouching dog as well). Later, dogs' pointing abilities were used to let gunners get closer, and be readier, for a shot.

Pointing dogs arose in continental Europe as well as in England. Today's pointing breeds are a varied and eclectic group sharing one key characteristic: the instinct to stop and freeze in the presence of gamebird scent.

The major advantage of a pointing dog is that it can hunt beyond gun range. A flushing spaniel or retriever must be kept close, so that the hunter can shoot any bird that the dog pushes out; by contrast, a pointing dog can be allowed to range more widely, cover more territory, use its own judgment to find birds wherever they may be. A good pointing dog seems to float through the cover, running effortlessly, moving from one likely place to the next—until it stops, sometimes almost skidding into a stance of utter immobility, eyes staring, limbs rigid, its whole body announcing that game is at hand.

In general, pointing dogs are more difficult to train than are flushing spaniels or retrievers. The pointer's is a more exacting task: to get close enough to a bird to scent it, yet not so close that the bird is frightened into flight. By nature, pointing dogs are more independent than spaniels and retrievers: they need to be, to strike out on their own and find game. Pointing dogs require lots of work, lots of exposure to birds under actual field conditions. While it is possible to hunt with a half-trained spaniel or retriever, a half-trained pointing dog will drive you to distraction by bumping distant birds and ignoring whistle commands (the dog having realized that it is too far away for you to apply instant discipline). Many people hunting with poorly trained pointers would actually be better served by flushing dogs.

The well-trained pointing dog is a bold hunter that nevertheless maintains contact with its handler and responds to directional commands. Where the country is open, the dog ranges ahead; where the cover is thick, it tightens its pattern. On point, the dog holds—remains "staunch"—as long as the bird stays put. If the bird runs, the dog may ease out of the point and cast ahead, freezing again when it hits hot scent. When the bird is finally pinned (confused or frightened enough that it stays put), the hunter walks in and flushes it.

A dog trained to maintain its point even after a bird is flushed and shot at is said to be "steady": It takes many hours of work to bring a dog to this level. A steady dog is a joy to hunt over. It can mark the bird for a retrieve. It is less likely to get shot by a hunter concentrating on a flushing gamebird. Most hunters settle for a dog that is staunch on point, and do not care if it is frequently not steady to flush or shot. A veteran hunter, Ray P. Holland, considers the matter in *Shotgunning in the Uplands:* "The shot-breaking dog generally gets to the crippled bird and stops him, while the well-trained pointer or setter, who stands and waits for the order to retrieve, works under a handicap. I don't like to have a dog dash out when a bird falls and flush other birds still in the cover while I stand there with an empty gun, but I can stand this rather than lose a bird with a broken wing."

In contrast to the spaniels and retrievers, who love to fetch, few pointing dogs are really keen about retrieving. Some hunters do not require their pointing dogs to fetch, and are satisfied if the canines simply point a dead bird. Such dogs will have trouble catching a cripple, however, because their instinct will tell them to hesitate before moving in and grabbing it. One way to train a pointing dog to retrieve is to first get the dog reliably staunch, and then force-train it to fetch. Force-training is a time-consuming, repetitious procedure in which mild pain is inflicted to persuade the dog to pick up, carry, and release objects on command. If the dog is taught to retrieve before it learns staunchness, it may never develop into a dependable pointer.

The pointing breeds are split into two groups. The first group, the setters (English, Irish, and Gordon) and the pointer, come to us from the British Isles and have been in North America for hundreds of years. The so-called versatile or continental breeds were imported from Europe primarily during this century: the Brittany, German shorthaired pointer, German wirehaired pointer, vizsla, Weimaraner, wirehaired pointing griffon, pudelpointer, and several others.

The two groups differ in appearance, hunting range and manner, strength of retrieving instinct, and willingness to enter water. The setters and the pointer have long tails, while the continentals all have their tails docked. The setters and the pointer typically are faster and range more widely, although some of the continental dogs reach out, too, especially those bred to run in field trials. The setters and the pointer rely mainly on body scent to locate birds; the continentals use body scent, but they also put their noses to the ground to puzzle out foot scent, slowing them down further. The setters and the pointer generally register a more striking, intense point. The continental breeds typically have stronger retrieving instincts and enter water more readily, although none of the pointing breeds take to the water as eagerly as spaniels and retrievers.

Pointing breeds can be expected to work all of the upland birds. They excel on birds that hold tightly: in the East and South, woodcock and quail; out West, sharp-tailed grouse, prairie chicken, and Hungarian partridge. Birds that run can give pointing dogs fits, particularly ruffed grouse and ring-necked pheasants, although savvy, well-trained pointing dogs ultimately do a masterful job even on these wary gamebirds. Some pointing dogs, especially the continentals, will fetch ducks from water, but none of the breeds have the coat for prolonged water work in frigid weather.

In my experience, a hunter will get more shots behind a flushing dog but will connect on a higher percentage of shots taken over a pointer, having more time to get ready before the bird goes up. In some hunting situations the wider range of the pointing dog will let it find more birds, yielding more overall opportunities. Many hunters get a supreme thrill out of watching a pointing dog glide and shift through cover, locate game, lock onto point—even if the bird ends up legging it away through the brush.

The English setter is a popular pointing breed, good-looking, affectionate, a traditional choice for ruffed grouse, woodcock, quail. The slower, more methodical Gordon setter has a handsome black-and-tan coat. The red-coated Irish setter has declined in popularity as a gun dog (many are bred for show or as pets), but the closely related red setter is a good hunter. The pointer is short-coated, lanky, hard-running, capable of reaching out in open country: a classic quail dog that will also hunt ruffed grouse, woodcock, and pheasant.

The Brittany is a short- to medium-range hunter effective in thick cover on woodcock and ruffed grouse; it is soft-natured and very friendly. The German shorthaired pointer has proven the most popular of the continental breeds: hardy, close-working, a practical gun dog that will retrieve. The German wirehaired pointer, or drahthaar, is a likeable, intelligent canine whose thick stiff coat sheds water and protects against thorns. Another German breed, the Weimaraner, has a low-maintenance silver-gray coat. The coppery-coated vizsla, from Hungary, works at a fairly close range, as does the wirehaired pointing griffon, an all-around hunter supported by an aggressive, effective breed club. The pudelpointer is a rare breed that will point upland game and also retrieve waterfowl. Other versatile Europeans (all extremely rare) include the large and small Munsterlanders, German longhaired pointer, and spinone.

Resources

Hunt Close!, Jerome B. Robinson. Winchester Press, New York, 1978.

Gun-Dog Training: Pointing Dogs, Kenneth Roebuck. Stackpole, Harrisburg, PA, 1983.

Training Pointing Dogs, Paul Long. Lyons & Burford, New York, 1985.

"Point" column, Charley Waterman. *Gun Dog* (bimonthly), Stover Publishing, P.O. Box 35098, Des Moines, IA 50315.

English
SETTER

*O*f *Englishe Dogges*, a sixteenth-century treatise by John Caius, physician to King Edward VI, distinguished between two types of land spaniels: One flushed game, the other pointed it. The kind that pointed was a "setter." "When he hath found the bird, he keepeth sure and fast silence, he stayeth his steps and will proceed no further and with a close, covert, watching eye, layeth his belly to the ground . . . The place being known by the means of the dog, the fowler immediately openeth and spreadeth his net."

The setter—also called a "setting spaniel"—reputedly was derived from spaniels that hesitated before flushing game. The probable spaniel origin is expressed in the breed's longish coat, happy and friendly nature, and willingness to splash through water while hunting.

The English setter emerged from a welter of setter types in early nineteenth-century England. Before that time, Gordon setters, Irish setters, and English setters were freely crossbred.

Good-looking and affectionate, the English setter is a traditional choice for ruffed grouse, wood-cock, and quail.

Around 1825, Edward Laverack of Whitchurch, Shropshire, in western England, began breeding a line of setters that gained widespread acceptance in both the hunting field and the show ring. Laverack's were large, robust dogs whose luxuriant coats had considerable feathering: flossy fur standing off from the chest, backs of the legs, and underside of the tail. Laverack is credited with standardizing the English setter; he is known as the "father of the breed." Well-heeled hunters in the United States bought dogs of his line and interbred them with "native" setter strains developed in this country from earlier importations.

In the 1860s, R. L. Purcell Llewellin of Pembrokeshire, South Wales, bought several dogs from Laverack and crossed them with setters from northern England to develop a smaller, faster, racier type than the Laverack, and a better hunting dog. Llewellin setters, too, were widely exported to America, where they won many field trials and became the rage among the sporting set in the late 1800s. To this day, the Field Dog Stud Book, the registry used by English setter owners who hunt or field-trial their dogs, recognizes Llewellins as a distinctive strain.

Most field-bred English setters in North America descend from early American lines with various blendings of Llewellin or Laverack genes. A bewildering number of types exist. There are large, robust setters and lean, sleek ones. Birdy, close-working, personal hunting dogs that point staunchly and retrieve downed birds, and high-strung, whip-thin racers bred to compete with pointers in field trial stakes, where dogs go so fast and so far that the judges follow on horseback. Show- and pet-stock setters—gangling, sluggish dogs unsuited to the game coverts—trace back to the Laverack lines.

The typical hunting English setter stands twenty-four inches at the shoulder and weighs fifty pounds—one step up in size from the English springer spaniel. Most setters are white-coated: Overlaid on this eye-catching background are patches of black or orange (actually a rich reddish tan); or black or orange "belton," a term for ticking coined by Laverack from the name of an English town where many setters shared this distinctive dappled pattern. Some setters are tricolor: white with black heads and tan eyebrows and cheek patches.

The English setter has a pleasant, loving disposition. It makes an excellent house pet, is gentle and mannerly, and just plain fun to be with. The setter wants to please its master, an attitude that keeps it working relatively near to the gun, checking in periodically so that it can go where the hunter wishes it to.

"In style and dash of ranging, in courage and capacity of covering ground; in beauty of form and grace of attitude; in variety of color and elegance of clothing," said Craven, a nineteenth-century British writer, "no animal of his species will at all bear comparison with him."

The modern English setter works pheasants, in weed fields or boggy thickets. It points woodcock solidly. The setter is an excellent quail dog. It does not take the heat as well as the pointer, nor does it have the pointer's stamina or speed; the latter is more suitable for quail in open country where the dog must range widely to check out many discrete patches of cover. But the setter will give splendid service in the tighter coverts—briars, honeysuckle, swampy bottoms—where bobwhites often shelter. On the prairies, the setter is a prime choice for hunting sage and sharp-tailed grouse, prairie chicken, and Hungarian partridge.

The English setter has long been the traditional pointing dog for ruffed grouse. Its heavy coat insulates against cold, and it does not mind crossing creeks or slogging through bogs. There are two schools of thought on what constitutes good grouse work. Some hunters favor a slow dog that will not scare a grouse into flushing wild. Other hunters want a faster dog that will startle the birds, cow them into freezing and holding under point;

they also want the dog to range widely and work independently, checking out more cover than the hunter could sample on foot. (In times past, it was harder to locate a dog locked up on point in a distant patch of slash or thornapples; now the modern setter may wear on its collar an electronic "bell" that will start beeping only when the dog stops moving.)

The English setter, perhaps because of its spaniel background, is more apt to fetch than the pointer, but less so than the continental breeds, and much less so than the spaniels and retrievers. Today, most authorities maintain that the English setter matures and learns more slowly than the pointer—but that the setter remembers its lessons longer and requires less brushing up. Apparently this wasn't always the case. Frank Forester, a leading sporting writer of the last century, credited the pointer with "greater retention of what he has learned, with less inclination to run riot and require partial rebreaking after he has long lain idle." Still, wrote Forester, "First in the list of sporting dogs, without a moment's hesitation, I place the setter."

Before buying a setter, decide if you want to hunt or field-trial the dog. If it's a hunting partner you want, improve your chances of getting a trainable partner (and avoiding a fast, extra-intense dog that will be a handful to train and to hunt over) by searching out solid hunting lines. Some of the best hunting setters come not from big-name kennels, which depend on field-trial wins for publicizing their lines, but from people who have real, in-the-field bird dogs and produce a litter only once every few years. Virtually all English setters in the American Kennel Club registry are from show and pet stock. Avoid them.

Summary: Medium size, with medium-long fur. Traditional choice for ruffed grouse; excels on prairie grouse, quail, woodcock. Stylish pointer; some will fetch. Pleasant and loving, thrives in the house. Trains more slowly than pointer, but retains lessons better. Some field-trial breeding too intense and fast for the average foot hunter.

Resources

The New Complete English Setter, Davis H. Tuck. Howell Book House, New York, 1982.

"Versatile English Setters," Jerome B. Robinson. *Sports Afield*, February 1987.

"The Llewellin Setter," Rick Van Etten. *Gun Dog*, March/ April 1988.

"The Ryman Setter," Rick Van Etten. *Gun Dog*, April/May 1991.

Irish
SETTER

I n *New England Grouse Shooting*, William Harnden Foster has a drawing of a market hunter from the last century. The man's dog is an Irish setter, as long, wiry, and rawboned as its bowler-hatted, mutton-chopped owner, who is running a rod down the right barrel of his muzzle-loading shotgun. A haze of burnt powder hangs in the air; the setter lies flat on its belly in the leaves, a downed grouse between its paws.

According to Foster, Irish setters were popular in the New England grouse coverts of the 1870s and 1880s. Foster describes these dogs as "hard to train and often hard to handle, but . . . once finished [they] were highly intelligent and capable." The nineteenth-century sporting writer Frank Forester wrote: "The points of the Irish setter are a more bony, angular, and wiry frame, a longer head, a less silky and straighter coat, than those of the English [setter]. His color ought to be a deep orange-red

Today's red setter carries on the hunting genes of yesterday's Irish setter.

and white; a common mark is a strip of white between the eyes, a white ring round the neck, white stockings, and a white tag to the tail."

Forester said Irish setters showed "a savage ferocity of temper, always extreme courage, high spirit, and indomitable pluck. They are naturally wild, and given to riot to the verge of indocility, require much breaking (I had almost said continual breaking) . . . and a tight hand over them. With these, they are of undeniable excellence."

Things have changed. Today's Irish setter—at least the Irish setter most of us see walking at leash—is a different beast, physically and mentally. Most Irish setters registered with the American Kennel Club have little or no hunting ability. Bred strictly for their appearance (which differs markedly from Forester's description above), they are flighty, difficult to train, and generally unimpressed by gamebirds.

Fortunately, a group of modern hunting dog fanciers have rescued the Irish setter from its handsome mediocrity, recreating a stylish, intelligent, trainable bird dog—which, because of cross-breeding with English setters to reinstate lost hunting instincts, looks much like the setter Forester described in the mid-1800s.

The pet- and show-stock Irish—which the hunter should studiously avoid—is a big, solid, heavy-boned dog with a chiseled, blocky head, excessive feathering, and a lustrous mahogany coat. It stands twenty-five inches or taller at the shoulder and weighs fifty to seventy-five pounds. It is registered with the American Kennel Club. (To be fair, a few AKC-registered purebred Irish setters are good hunters, but they are very rare.)

Today's hunting Irish, widely known as the "red setter," is registered with the Field Dog Stud Book, the standard registry for working pointing dogs. The red setter—created by the English cross—is a smaller, leaner specimen than its bench-bred cousin.

Its muzzle is less massive, its ears shorter and set higher on the head. Twenty to twenty-four inches tall, it weighs about forty-five pounds. Where the show-stock Irish runs with a heavy, labored gallop, the red setter covers ground with a beautiful fluid gait. Its coat is a lighter shade of red: a russet or fawn color, often with white on the paws, chest, and face—like the traditional setter bred from the 1600s in Ireland, the Irish setter of Frank Forester's day. (Interestingly, in 1878 the American Kennel Club stud book included Irish setters that were lemon, black, black-and-white, and red-and-white, as well as solid red.)

The red setter is quite trainable and learns more quickly and at a younger age than the Irish setter of a century past. The dog responds best to gentle, firm handling. Most red setters point with great intensity and a high tail. The red setter has a keen, accurate nose and possesses good stamina.

The red setter has already made a mark in field trials. Yet, according to Bob Sprouse, who edits *The Flushing Whip*, the National Red Setter Field Trial Club bulletin, eighty percent of club members are bird hunters and do not trial their dogs. "A lot of breeders," he says, "concentrate on developing walking gun dogs."

Affectionate and sensible, red setters make good house pets. Those bred in the West tend to be naturally bigger-running dogs, to help them cover large chunks of open territory and find widely spaced birds. Eastern red setters, on the other hand, are apt to work closer to the hunter in the region's thick, fragmented coverts. Red setters can be expected to work all the upland gamebirds.

W. E. "Ned" LeGrande, from Douglassville, Pennsylvania, is considered the father of the modern red setter. In the 1950s LeGrande and some friends formed the National Red Setter Field Trial Club. They searched out real hunting Irish setters, including several from a strain originally used on prairie chickens in Minnesota, and bred them to red-and-white English setters. A key dog in this restoration was Askew's Carolina Lady, an Irish setter bitch discovered on a farm in North Carolina; her owner had decided to part with her, it is said, because of her penchant for "biting ladies." Despite this flaw, Lady was an excellent hunting and trial dog who passed on her field traits to her offspring. (Her likeness now decorates the logo of the National Red Setter Field Trial Club.)

LeGrande reportedly spent a small fortune buying and breeding the best field Irish setters in North America; he also imported dogs from Ireland. By closely controlling all English setter additions, LeGrande and his partners were able to limit the amount of white in the red setter's coat while strengthening hunting and pointing instincts. Later, after three generations of pure Irish setter ancestry had once again been established, the Field Dog Stud Book allowed red setter owners to register their dogs as purebred Irish setters—which, of course, stirred up controversy among owners of Irish setters registered with the American Kennel Club.

Says one red setter enthusiast, "Criticism doesn't matter. Fifty years from now nobody will remember what we did. They'll only know that Irish setters are good hunting dogs."

Summary: Medium to large; long-haired. Points all upland birds. Recently restored "red setter" an excellent hunting strain; vast majority of AKC-registered Irish will not hunt. Red setter biddable, learns quickly. Good house pet.

Resources

"The 'New' Irish—A Tradition Lives On," Rick Van Etten. *Gun Dog*, November/December 1983.

"The Red Setter: A Dog of a (Slightly) Different Color," Rick Van Etten. *Gun Dog*, March/April 1987.

The Flushing Whip, National Red Setter Field Trial Club, Bob Sprouse, ed., 16607 W. Moline-Martin Rd., Graytown, OH 43432.

Gordon
SETTER

The Gordon setter is, in many ways, a dog of the last century. In the late 1800s it was a favorite among market hunters supplying game to the restaurant trade. It earned a reputation as a "meat dog": not flashy, a steady, durable performer that could fill the game bag day after day. Too, it was the gentleman's shooting dog, the thorough worker that combed the cover at a pace comfortable for a hunter on foot.

As Scotland's contribution to the British setter triumverate, the Gordon is brawnier than either the English or the Irish setter; it is a big, strong, black-and-tan dog. Wealthy landowners in Scotland and northern England developed the breed to hunt grouse on the moors. Historians credit the fourth Duke of Gordon with establishing a genetically distinct type in the late 1700s; at that time the dog was called the Gordon Castle setter. Legend has it that the Duke shaped his strain by crossing setters with bloodhounds and at least one black-and-tan collie—a bitch named Maddy, who, it was said, upon smelling game would stop and "watch" it.

The hunter charmed by the Gordon setter's dark beauty must be sure to choose a puppy out of solid field stock.

The statesman Daniel Webster and his hunting partner George Blunt brought the first recorded Gordons to America in 1842—a male named Rake and a female, Rachel. The breed's reputation quickly spread. "Vying with the Irish setter and his English cousin for popularity as the grouse dog of three generations ago was the Gordon," wrote William Harnden Foster in *New England Grouse Shooting*, published in 1947. "The Gordon was a level-headed, methodical, tireless worker that produced excellent results. Although many of our younger generation of grouse hunters have never seen a Gordon in the field, he had his day—a day that ended only when grouse became more scarce and more wary, and dogs of greater speed and range . . . replaced the handsome, honest, black-and-tan setter."

Field trials also diminished the Gordon by rewarding faster and more dramatic performers. While field trialers and hunters were falling out of love with the Gordon, show people were admiring the breed's dark beauty. With little or no regard for hunting abilities or intelligence, they began breeding Gordons, exaggerating certain traits: long, flossy feathering; a heavily flewed muzzle; a coat that was free of white hair; and, to catch a show judge's eye, a bulkier, heavier build. In 1963 the Gordon Setter Club of America persuaded the American Kennel Club to change the official breed standard to allow dogs that weighed nearly twice as much as the original Gordon gun dogs. The new Gordons were clumsy beasts that could not negotiate hunting cover; they did not point intensely and were apt to play, rather than work, in the field. The situation grew so bleak that in 1967, Philip Rice and John Dahl wrote in their book, *Hunting Dogs*, "Finding a Gordon setter puppy who is fairly sure to develop into an adult with speed, staunchness on point, and bird-finding ability is practically out of the question."

Fortunately, a few kennels—most of them small rural operations whose owners nurtured fond memories of the steady, elegant Gordons of years gone by—kept producing the old-style gun-dog stock. Thanks to these steadfast enthusiasts (and probably the covert addition of English setter genes), an effective modern hunting Gordon has emerged over the last decade. For someone daunted by today's hard-going English setters, the Gordon provides a good-looking traditional alternative to the short-tailed continental breeds. The Gordon is a legitimate choice for smaller grouse and woodcock coverts, for thick pheasant fields, and for tangled bottomlands where quail hide.

The largest concentration of field-bred Gordons is in California. The East Coast, Canada, the Southwest, the Pacific Northwest, and Hawaii also have Gordon setter field trial clubs. Owners of field-type Gordons have established a National Gordon Setter Association, affiliated with the Field Dog Stud Book in Chicago. The association sponsors field trials where Gordons compete against excellent bird dogs of all breeds. (The show-oriented Gordon Setter Club of America remains linked with the American Kennel Club in New York.)

Today's field-bred Gordon stands twenty-four or twenty-five inches at the shoulder and weighs forty-five to fifty-five pounds; a show dog may be twenty-seven inches and eighty pounds. The coat is predominantly black, with rich rusty tan accents on the chest, legs, feet, stern, and a dot above each eye. Field-type dogs may have a white splash on the chest, taboo for show Gordons. The fur—long, smooth, and silky—protects against thorns but attracts burs and sticktights.

One of the longstanding complaints about the Gordon is that its dark coat is hard to spot in thick cover. Actually, many Gordon owners report that the dog's relatively close hunting range, plus its habit of frequently checking in on its master, give the hunter a good idea of where the dog will be. And against dry grass or snow, the dark coat shows up nicely.

In the field, the Gordon has stamina, endurance, and an innate tendency to pace itself. It is the kind of dog that, if in shape, can be taken hunting four or five days in a row. Some believe the Gordon's nose is unrivaled among hunting dogs. The breed has a soft mouth and a natural desire to fetch. Most Gordons take to water readily and can be used for occasional warm-weather duck retrieving. On point, Gordons tend to be "looser" than the pointer and the English setter, which become more rigid. A Gordon may glance away from a bird to look at the approaching hunter; the dog is apt to break point if the bird runs off, loop out in front, and reestablish point farther on.

Gordons are excellent family dogs, calm and good with children. Most are one-person or one-family dogs, needing plenty of attention. If you plan to train a dog yourself, a Gordon is a forgiving breed that can bounce back from a novice's mistakes. Although tough and somewhat independent-minded, the Gordon wants to please. It learns quickly, and once trained needs little repetition. If you expect to send your dog to a professional trainer, a Gordon is not a good choice, unless your trainer has experience with the breed.

Suzanne and Norman Sorby of Petaluma, California, run Springset Kennel, the largest and foremost Gordon setter operation in the country, turning out around three hundred gun-dog pups each year, over half of which are sent outside the state. Springset Gordons have won field trials, shoot-to-retrieve competitions, and even some show events. They are reputed to be calm, biddable workers. The Sorbys do not kennel their Gordons individually, believing the breed does best when unconfined. Thirty to forty dogs run loose on the Sorbys' lawn and sleep together in a common room. Before morning training sessions, a sea of black and tan flows about Norman Sorby while he calls off the names of eight or ten dogs he plans to work. When a dog hears its name, it steps forward and jumps onto the trailer.

Summary: Medium to large, dark-coated, slow-paced worker on all upland birds. Medium to close range; good choice for smaller coverts. Excellent nose. May show a "loose," less-than-stylish point. Fur snarls with burs. Show stock predominates, but hunting lines also exist. One-person dog best trained by owner; learns quickly, easily trained by novice, strong desire to please. Not a kennel dog; needs plenty of attention.

Resources

The Field Gordon Setter, Suzanne and Norman Sorby. Springset Gordon Setter Kennels, Petaluma, California, 1987.

"From Within the Tangles—the Gordon Setter," Jerry Warrington. *Gun Dog*, July/August 1982.

"The Gordon Setter: Big, Beautiful, Birdy," Rick Penn. *Gun Dog*, May/June 1984.

"Gordons: The Other Setter," J. L. Wagner. *Gun Dog*, August/September 1990.

National Gordon Setter Association, Jean De Streel, 712 Wolf Avenue, Easton, PA 18042.

Pointer

You see the advertisement in a hunting magazine, a kennel with an address south of the Mason-Dixon line selling "bird dogs" —no other name, just "bird dogs," and even without a picture you know beyond a doubt that the breed in reference is the pointer.

The pointer has been called "the paragon of the pointing breeds," "a no-nonsense dog," and "a hunting machine." It is the top choice of professional field trialers and of commercial shooting preserves that run strings of dogs and run them hard. The pointer is tough, spirited, hard-charging, handsome—a classy canine that can meet the demands of any upland gamebird in any type of cover.

The pointer arose in England in the sixteenth and seventeenth centuries when the English apparently brought in pointing dogs from Europe, including the Spanish pointer, and crossed them with foxhounds and "setting spaniels." To this day many Americans refer to the "English pointer," perhaps not realizing that the breed flowered here in North America, where U.S. and Canadian

In the South, the pointer is the breed of choice for quail; it also works well on grouse.

hunters developed the pointer into a dog that could reach out and handle the wide open spaces and large blocks of cover then prevalent on our continent.

In the late 1800s, when the pointer first began gaining wide popularity in America, it faced stiff competition from the English setter. Setters dominated field trials and were considered the premier hunting dogs. Not until the turn of the century were pointers even allowed to compete in the same trials as setters. But around 1910, pointers began beating setters in major trials run on quail and prairie chicken. Pointers proved themselves faster than setters, and generally found more birds. They matured more quickly and were better able to accept strict, even harsh, discipline. Before long, the pointer ousted the setter as the top trial dog, and it has set the standard ever since. More important, it excels in the game coverts.

The pointer is a medium to medium-large dog, twenty-four or twenty-five inches at the shoulder, fifty to sixty pounds, with a lean, streamlined physique. The thin skin reveals rippling muscles and sculpted bone. The coat is flat, short, and dense. It does not pick up burs and sticktights.

Briars can be hard on a thin-skinned dog: Some hunters protect their pointers' tails by wrapping them with duct tape. And the pointer suffers more than the fuller-coated dog when the weather turns bitter. Charley Waterman, pointing dog columnist for *Gun Dog* magazine, writes: "I have found that somewhere around zero degrees my English pointers [begin] to lose efficiency. . . . Actually, I don't think too many bird hunters operate at much below zero very often." Asserts Waterman, "Heat has stopped more bird dogs than cold"—and in the hot and dry, the pointer can go longer than any other breed.

White with liver patches is the most common color scheme; pointers are also white-and-black, white-and-lemon, or solid white, sometimes with ticking, always readily visible in the field. The head somewhat suggests a hound's profile: a squared-off muzzle, a prominent stop (the change in angle where the brow breaks upward from the muzzle), a broad dome, and high-set, thin-leathered ears.

William Harnden Foster, in his 1947 *New England Grouse Shooting*, noted that for many years hunters of that region placed a premium on pointers having a so-called split nose, an abnormally deep crease that reached from the mouth upward and practically separated the nostrils; such dogs were supposed to have vastly superior scenting ability.

The pointer's expression is alert, keen, intelligent. It tends to be a businesslike breed, and its business is, quite simply, birds. According to Dave Duffey, who has trained many gun dogs of all breeds, "If you know hounds and horses, you'll get along well with a pointer. If your experience has been with spaniels or retrievers, you'll have to do some adjusting." Although it will have a good disposition, the average pointer will not be demonstrative. Greeting its master with a few tail wags rather than a setter's overflowing joy, it will be more concerned with getting onto the training field or hunting ground. Some pointers make excellent house pets. Most adapt readily to kennel life, not needing as much attention and affection as other breeds.

Pointers show abundant pointing and backing instinct (a dog "backs" when, after noticing another dog on point, it honors the first dog by going on point itself), and they show it quickly, taking to training at a young age. If you buy a pup in the spring—and if you are a good trainer, putting in lots of time with your dog—you may well have a hunting companion by fall. If, on the other hand, you are an inexperienced trainer, tend to be indecisive, and find that disciplining a dog goes against your grain—you will in all likelihood do a better job with a softer, slower-developing breed like the English setter. Pointers require lots of field work and experience on live birds to become, and to remain, good cooperative hunters.

A hard-driving pointer is a beautiful animal to behold. It gobbles up the ground, muscles flexing, hindquarters bunching and thrusting in a display of speed, power, and boldness. When it hits scent, it will point intensely, often with the tail straight up. (That's the fashion now; in the last century hunters preferred the tail straight out in back.)

A pointer can be a tremendous bird-finder because it covers so much ground: Experts estimate that a big-running pointer may go a hundred miles on a long day's hunt. But many hunters are scared off by the pointer's fire. In open country the dog may hunt out to a quarter or even a half mile; in thick, restricted cover it will tighten up and keep in contact with the hunter, but it will still be farther out, and moving faster, than an English setter or one of the continental breeds. The average pointer can, in fact, be too much bird dog for many hunters: so fast and full of energy that when the dog smells birds, the hunter loses control of the situation.

Pointers do their best work on covey-type birds that hold rather than run. In the northern plains they excel on sharp-tailed grouse, Hungarian partridge, and prairie chicken. They hunt pheasants, but, like all the pointing breeds, sometimes have difficulties with these skulking, running gamebirds.

The pointer is the top choice for hunting bobwhite quail. It is *the* breed in the South, where hunters follow it on foot, on horseback, or in wagons. The dogs work the edges of cultivated fields, checking for scent left by coveys that have left the shelter of bordering brushlands and fed into the fields. Then, on the way to the next field, they close in and hunt the intervening woods or thickets.

Some of the best grouse dogs are pointers. They may be fleet, slashing performers that "pin" their birds with a swift, aggressive approach. Or, given a different training regimen or springing from a different breeding line, they may be closer-working, less-flamboyant shooting dogs. There is a movement toward pointers among grouse and woodcock hunters today as more and more pointers win field trials run on these two birds.

As an all-around performer in the grouse coverts, an English setter would seem to hold one advantage over the pointer: It is a bit more inclined to retrieve, although the pointer can be taught to fetch if properly introduced and trained. Foster, in *New England Grouse Shooting*, found little to rank the English setter—tradition's choice—above the pointer, or vice versa. "A good one from either breed is preferable to a second-rater from the other," he wrote.

If you hunt small, restricted coverts—a pheasant field next to a housing development, a woodcock bottom near a busy road, a grouse thicket surrounded by posted land—a pointer will not suit you as well as a closer-working, more highly controlled dog, such as one of the continental breeds developed in Europe for precisely that sort of hunting. But if your coverts are big and expansive, and if you have the time and temperament to properly train it, the pointer has the potential to become a "superior" hunter—the epitome of a bird dog.

Summary: Medium to large, short-haired, points all upland birds, first choice for bobwhite quail. Good in hot conditions. Tends to run fast, range widely; top field-trial breed. Most will not retrieve. Needs firm, frequent training; shows potential early and hunts at a young age. Not a good first dog. Adapts well to living in kennel; requires less personal attention and affection than other breeds.

Resources

"The Misunderstood Breed," Nick Sisley. *Hunting Dog*, July 1971.

"Pointer," Dave Duffey. *Gun Dog*, July/August 1989.

The Brittany, widely used on woodcock, ruffed grouse, and pheasants, makes an excellent first dog.

Brittany

F rank Forester was a well-known writer about upland hunting in the nineteenth century. He liked to gun behind the wide-ranging pointers and setters of his day, but made no bones about their limitations in thick cover: "They will, in covert, range entirely out of shot, will probably overrun and put up many birds quite beyond the shooter's range, or, coming to a dead point at a quarter of a mile's distance, with heaven knows how much brush and brier intervening, will be missing half of the time, or will have instead of themselves hunting, to be painfully hunted up by their owner."

Forester did not have available to him a sturdy, persevering, keen-nosed, close-working little pointing dog that many North American hunters today confidently take into the thickets after pheasant, woodcock, and grouse: the Brittany.

Up until the 1980s the breed was known as the Brittany spaniel: the only spaniel to point instead of flush its game. Now it is called simply Brittany, to separate it from the flushing spaniels and to commemorate its place of origin. Spaniels had long flourished on the Brittany peninsula on the northwest coast of France.

In the mid-1800s, locals began crossing their smallish flushing dogs with English, Irish, and Gordon setters owned by wealthy sportsmen from the British Isles who were drawn by the region's superb woodcock hunting. Other breeds—the red-and-white Welsh springer spaniel, the pointer, and unspecified hounds—may also have been added. What arose was a serviceable hunting dog expressing virtues of both setters and spaniels: A dog that would instinctively point and also retrieve.

We have a description by a French army veterinarian, Major P. Grand-Chavin: "In 1906 I arrived in garrison at Pontivy. . . . In traveling through villages I noticed the presence of many small spaniels. Almost all had short tails, the ears looked pretty much the same and they were colored white-chestnut, white-orange, and white-black. These small animals were fascinating due to a lively physiognomy, a short gait, and intelligent looks. Every-where people would tell me they were excellent hunters, fearless of the thicket, would point very well, and especially well did they hunt the hare. . . . Their endurance and rusticity were often revealed to me during the course of the long hunting days in a country much intersected with rivers and canals and often very woody."

By 1900 a definite type had emerged, and in 1907 a group of French sportsmen founded a Brittany spaniel club and adopted a breed standard. In 1931, Louis Thebaud of Morristown, New Jersey, brought the first Brittany to the United States. Today it is one of the most popular pointing breeds in North America.

The Brittany stands seventeen and a half to twenty and a half inches and weighs thirty to forty pounds—compact enough to negotiate thick cover. The slightly wavy coat, of medium length, gives good protection against thorns. Most Brittanys are colored white with orange patches or white with liver patches; usually there is some ticking.

The head is similar to that of the English setter, except shorter, broader across the dome, and with the ears set higher. The over-all expression is alert, intelligent, friendly, a bit raffish. The Brit-tany shows a distinctive "downhill" body profile: strong shoulders and chest above a pair of longish front legs, and a stout back that slopes down to a solid rear end atop shorter hind legs.

Some Brittanys are born with a naturally short tail, others with a longer tail that requires docking; either way, the appendage ends up about four inches long. The advantage of a short tail is that its tip does not get slashed and bloodied in the brush. Inter-estingly, the 1907 French breed standard required the Brittany to have a naturally short tail; however, so many otherwise-normal Brittanys were born with long tails that the requirement was dropped.

The Brittany has a stable, biddable disposition. A good com-panion, noted for the bond it develops with its master, it much prefers the house to the kennel. Friendly and affectionate, it can also display an independence bordering on aloofness. There are hard Brittanys and soft Brittanys, but most are fairly sensitive by nature and respond best to repetition and coaxing during train-ing. The breed can accept mild punishment such as scolding, shaking, and an occasional rap on the nose with a forefinger. Harsher measures can ruin a Brittany. With a pup out of hunting stock and some work on the owner's part, one can have a Brittany doing good work on birds in less than a year.

The Brittany's strong suit is its tendency to remain close to the gun in thick cover, although it will move out to a longer range where the country opens up. The dog will thoroughly check the likeliest looking patches, hunting at a steady, lively pace, consis-tently keeping in touch with the hunter. Most Brittanys have ex-cellent noses and seldom miss game. A finished Brittany should be obedient; hunt within a range suitable to the cover; point staunchly; honor another dog's point; "hunt dead," or search for a downed bird on the hunter's say-so; and retrieve shot birds. Most like to fetch and, if properly trained, can be expected to retrieve all of the upland birds, doves, and even ducks out of the water.

The close-ranging Brittany is a top choice for ruffed grouse and woodcock in the thick coverts of the Northeast and the upper Midwest. The average Brittany is easier to train to hunt these two gamebirds than is the average pointer or setter; it seems especially able to cope with the flighty wariness of grouse. The Brittany also does reasonably well on pheasants. Although the classic Brittany lacks the stamina or range to perform as a big-running covey dog on quail, it does excellent work in the thick cover to which today's bobwhites often resort. It hunts sharp-tailed grouse, prairie chickens, and Hungarian partridge, doing its best work in tight, restricted places.

When the Brittany was introduced in the 1930s, Americans were used to stylish, wide-ranging dogs. The Brittany, some said, hunted too close, was too much "under foot." By the 1970s a bigger, leggier, harder-running Brittany had emerged, bred to compete with pointers and setters in field trials—a far cry from the comfortable, close-range bird dog that many upland gunners had come to cherish. According to David Follansbee, writing in 1979, "The Brittany in America has become incredibly variable in pattern, incredibly erratic in range, so that the foot hunter, in buying a puppy, is, as the French would say, 'playing roulette.'"

Another factor that can make it hard to find a good hunting puppy is the large number of Brittanys being bred as pets. Charley Waterman, columnist in *Gun Dog* magazine, writes: "If I were shopping for a Brittany I'd be very careful not to get into the non-hunting pet circles. At present, the hunting and pure-pet lines aren't firmly drawn."

A small but growing cadre of Brittany fanciers have returned to France for reliably close-working dogs. These so-called French Brittanys are distinctly different from the American type. Some of the French dogs have black noses (instead of brown or liver); some have black-and-white coats, and some are tricolor (white, orange, and black), combinations that place the dogs outside the American Kennel Club's standard. Enough French Brittanys have reached the United States that litters are frequently advertised in magazines such as *Gun Dog*.

In France, the Brittany is expected to adjust its range to suit the cover, and maintain close contact with the hunter. Those that compete in field trials work on wild birds under actual foot-hunting conditions. (In most American trials, the dogs are followed on horseback.) According to their proponents, French Brittanys are more alert, enthusiastic, and intelligent than their American counterparts: versatile, biddable throwbacks to the dogs that emerged from a welter of breeds on the Brittany peninsula almost a century past.

Summary: Small to medium size; naturally short or docked tail, medium-length coat. Good on grouse, woodcock, quail, pheasant, chukar. Strong retrieving instinct. Most work close to hunter, although field-trial dogs may range widely. Affectionate, biddable, require mild training regimen. Develop quickly, hunt at a young age. Excellent first dog for inexperienced trainer.

Resources

Training and Hunting the Brittany Spaniel, Ralph B. Hammond and Robert D. Hammond. A. S. Barnes, South Brunswick, NJ, 1971.

The New Complete Brittany, Maxwell Riddle. Howell Book House, New York, 1987.

"Revelation! The French Brittany," David Follansbee. *Gun Dog*, September/October 1982.

"A Texan Talks Up Brittanys," Max Oelschlaeger. *Gun Dog*, January/February 1987.

"The Brittany: Popular for a Good Reason," Rick Van Etten. *Gun Dog*, September/October 1988.

The American Brittany Club: 1392 Big Bethel Rd., Hampton, VA 23666.

German Shorthaired Pointer
(DEUTSCH KURZHAAR)

In 1925 a Montana physician, Charles Thornton, read a magazine article about German shorthaired pointers and decided he had to have these all-purpose hunters. Over the years, Thornton imported many dogs from top bloodlines. He used his shorthairs to point birds, herd cattle, fetch ducks, and tree raccoons. The breed caught on quickly with bird hunters in other western states, in Minnesota and Wisconsin, and in California. Today the German shorthair is widely used across North America, where it is the most popular of the continental pointing breeds.

The breed was created in Germany in the 1800s by hunters of the upper middle class, who, in the wake of political and social reforms, were newly able to lease and hunt on preserves and other lands formerly controlled by royalty. These hunters wanted a dog to do it all: point, trail wounded game, retrieve from land

The popular German shorthaired pointer is a hardy, close-working, practical gun dog that likes to retrieve.

and water, hunt rabbits and hares as well as birds, scent-trail big game, and even kill predators such as foxes. So, in a rational Teutonic manner, the hunters conferred, set goals, crossed stock from several breeds, field-tested the resulting dogs against a written standard—and kept breeding the best to the best. The Deutsche kurzhaarige vorstehund, or German shorthaired pointer, arose from a blending of the old Spanish pointer, the old German pointer, German scent hounds, and probably the French braque. Later, the English version of the pointer (itself a product of the Spanish pointer, foxhound, and English setter) was added to improve scenting powers and strengthen bird-handling ability.

The German shorthaired pointer developed into a steady, thorough, competent hunting dog. It has a superb nose and a deep-seated pointing instinct. It will hunt a variety of species—working close to the gun and maintaining contact with its handler—and retrieve shot game.

A large, sturdy dog (twenty-one to twenty-five inches at the shoulder and forty-five to seventy pounds), the shorthair is streamlined, barrel-chested, and well-muscled. Large leathery ears are set high on the sculpted head. The tail is docked back to about a third of its natural length.

The short, stiff, dense coat requires little maintenance. It turns aside briars better than a pointer's coat and sheds water better than a setter's; it does not pick up burs and sticktights. A fine, dense undercoat wards off the cold. Colors are liver and white, in several combinations: solid liver, liver with white patches, liver with white patches and ticking, white with liver patches and ticking.

Shorthairs learn quickly and develop a bit earlier than pointers and setters. Most will do good work in the field with a minimum of formal training. Intelligent, friendly, and even-tempered, they are less affected than other breeds by beginning trainers' mistakes. The shorthair makes a good first pointing dog: A hunter can stick with shorthairs if they suit his style of hunting, or, the next time around, move on to a swifter, more dashing breed that is harder to train. In the home, the shorthair makes an affectionate pet and an alert watchdog, although it may prove a bit big for close quarters.

The Germans developed the shorthair not for extremes of range or speed, but to carefully and methodically comb small tracts of cover. One factor automatically reining it in is its instinctive searching (thanks to its hound background) for foot scent as well as body scent of game. A good shorthair will keep close in a thicket, then push farther out where vegetation is patchy or sparse. Since it will not be dashing through the cover or making long casts, it will husband its strength and be able to hunt steadily and effectively all day. Shorthairs quarter naturally and require little directing in the field. Some, it must be admitted, are boot-polishers who hunt too close to the gun; others, bred to compete in field trials, are big-running dogs. But most shorthairs hunt at an effective range and at a pace comfortable for the average upland hunter.

The continental breeds are also known as the "versatile breeds," and the shorthair is as versatile as any. An excellent grouse and woodcock dog, it will work brushy fields, wet bottoms, and logging slash. It will do a good job on pheasants in limited coverts such as cattail swamps bordering cropland, weed patches near roads, and farm fields enclosed by posted land. It can be used on snipe and rails, and to retrieve ducks. While it can be hunted on open-cover game such as quail, chukar, Hungarian partridge, sharp-tailed grouse, sage grouse, and prairie chickens, one of the wider-ranging breeds—an English setter or a pointer—will cover more ground and find more birds. A shorthair will point rabbits, although few North American sportsmen encourage their dogs to do this.

Why do commercial shooting preserves use more German shorthairs than any other breed? The dogs are obedient and easily worked by different handlers, they are great bird finders, they trail cripples and retrieve shot birds. The shorthair is more inclined to fetch than the pointer or setter. It will not point as intensely as these two other breeds, which, coupled with its lack of a long tail, puts some hunters off.

German shorthairs may be registered with the American Kennel Club or the Field Dog Stud Book or both. Some are bred strictly for show or as pets and may lack hunting instincts. Around sixty-five local shorthair clubs exist in the United States. Most have annual field trials, and some sponsor hunting tests, specialty shows, and obedience trials. A separate group, Klub Deutsch Kurzhaar—USA (an American branch of a large German organization), conducts strict testing and will qualify for breeding only those dogs that are physically sound and demonstrate hunting skills and the ability to be handled in the field.

In the late 1930s a cadre of Midwestern shorthair owners decided to form a national breed club. They applied to the American Kennel Club for recognition. The group wanted to call itself the German Shorthair Pointer-Retriever Club of America. The AKC granted recognition but balked at the name: The German shorthair, it ruled, could be called a pointer or a retriever, but not both. A pity. The shorthair capably carries out both these tasks— and many more.

Summary: Medium to large, sturdy. Thorough hunter, medium range. Tracks, points, retrieves. Hunts all upland birds; can do limited duck retrieving if water not too cold. Good dove retriever. Short coat needs little maintenance, turns aside burs, thorns. Obedient; excellent choice for beginning trainer. Good house pet, although may be too large for some homes.

Resources

The Complete German Shorthaired Pointer, Fritz Seiger and Dr. F. von Dewitz-Coeltin. Denlinger, Fairfax, VA, 1951.

The New German Shorthaired Pointer, C. Bede Maxwell. Howell Book House, New York, 1963.

"This is the Shorthair," Parts I and II, Jim McCue. *Gun Dog*, March/April, May/June 1983.

German Shorthaired Pointer Club of America: Kenneth W. Clemons, 1031 Amy Belle Rd., Germantown, WI 53022.

Klub Deutsch Kurzhaar—USA: Herbert G. Hasemann, 7619 Oak Leaf Dr., Santa Rosa, CA 95409.

German Wirehaired Pointer
(DEUTSCH DRAHTHAAR)

The German wirehaired pointer, or Deutsch drahthaar, arose in Germany during the last quarter of the nineteenth century, an era of widespread experimentation in animal breeding. It derived from crosses between the wirehaired pointing griffon (a French breed); the pudelpointer (a cross between the poodle and the pointer); the stichelhaar (itself a product of four breeds: pointer, foxhound, pudelpointer, and Polish water dog); and the German shorthair, in an effort to produce a versatile dog for the foot hunter. Although a rather eclectic combination of genes, apparently it was an effective one: Some experts judge the wirehair the best of the many continental breeds imported to North America.

Yet even though it ranks as the top hunting dog in its native land, the German wirehair has never caught on here in a big way. The reason? Probably its appearance. Its coat, so practical in the black-

The drahthaar has a keen nose, good hunting desire, and a wire coat that sheds water and protects against thorns.

berry tangle and the cattail slough, is not considered classically beautiful. It lacks the setter's glossy softness that seemingly begs to be petted, nor does it show off the animal's musculature as dramatically as the pointer's sleek, thin coat does. Yet the wirehair's distinctive fur is a more practical covering than either.

The wirehair actually has two coats. Outermost is a layer of hard, coarse, flat-lying hair, three-quarters to one and a half inches long, to repel water and thorns. Beneath this layer is a dense undercoat that insulates in cold weather and is shed in warm weather, letting the wirehair adapt to almost any climate.

According to wirehair enthusiast Buz Fawcett, in an article in *Gun Dog* magazine, about half of the offspring in a typical litter will have acceptable wire coats. The other pups will go unregistered and be sold as pets at reduced prices. A wirehair with blonde or straw coloration will probably lack the wire coat. Acceptable colors are solid liver or liver with white spots or ticking, which gives a dappled gray-brown effect. Wirehair pups are born mostly white, with liver spots; with each coat change (up to eight in the first two years), they darken by gaining more liver in the white areas. As adults they resemble rough-coated German shorthairs with bristling eyebrows and fur on the muzzle like a beard.

The wirehair is about the same size as the shorthair, perhaps a bit leggier: males, twenty-four to twenty-six and a half inches; females, twenty-two to twenty-four and a half inches. Weights range from fifty to seventy pounds. The wire coat, although prominent, does not completely obscure the body's sturdy, strong-looking lines. The back is short and straight with a faint slope from front- to hindquarters; the tail, docked to about six inches, is carried horizontally or at a slight upward angle.

The foregoing describes the type of wirehair most often seen and the one most breeders strive for. In fact, there is great variation in the breed. You can find wirehairs that look almost exactly like German shorthairs, with little or no facial hair; or wirehairs with extremely thick coats, great bushy eyebrows, and flowing moustaches and beards. They can be slim and graceful or stocky and powerful.

Temperament also varies, from quietly personable to dangerously aggressive. (Wirehairs were used as guard dogs, along with Alsatians, Dobermans, and Rottweilers, by the German armed forces in World War II.) Wirehair enthusiast Fawcett notes that the majority of good wirehairs in this country have "excellent, if intense, personalities." The breed has a reputation for a lively intelligence that surfaces in occasional prankishness.

Although the breed is sometimes characterized as "aloof" and "independent," most wirehairs show plenty of affection to their owners. They are sometimes labeled one-family dogs. Most do better as household pets than as kennel dwellers: Some wirehairs, confined, become aggressive.

Many wirehairs are precocious, and some will be ready to have birds shot over them at the age of four to six months. Writes Fawcett, "They are undoubtedly the easiest hunting dog there is to train. . . . Unfortunately, when they've learned what you require and find out you want them to repeat the same skill over and over for the rest of their lives, they are shocked. Learning is fun. Repetition is boredom. The incautious handler will find his 'perfect' dog changing the rules or inventing new games with alarming frequency." Fawcett continues, "You'll find training is a lifetime activity if you're to keep your canine companion entertained."

Most wirehairs have excellent noses and a strong instinct to point and retrieve. They are keen hunters. Quicker and livelier afield than most of the other continentals, they nonetheless show good stamina. Their point may be less intense than that of a setter or pointer, and has been described as "businesslike." Most wirehairs hunt at a close to moderate range, adjusting naturally to the density of the cover.

In Germany, wirehairs are called Deutsch drahthaars and are closely tested and evaluated before their owners are allowed to breed them. In the field they are expected to find and hold game of any size (from hares to wild boars), track wounded game, point birds and retrieve them from land and water, and be good and loyal companions. In North America we generally ask them to perform the latter two tasks. They are adaptable, versatile dogs geared to the hunter on foot. They can handle any of the upland birds and retrieve from water under all but the most severe conditions. Wirehairs have built an excellent reputation as pheasant dogs, and commercial preserves use many of them.

The wirehair did not gain official recognition in Germany until 1928, even though it had been the top sporting dog in that country for many years. The breed spread throughout Europe in the early 1930s and became the most popular hunting dog in Scandinavia. When brought to North America in the 1930s, and for several decades thereafter, the breed was known as the drahthaar, the German word for wirehair. The American Kennel Club's official name is German wirehaired pointer.

Verein Deutsch-Drahthaar (VDD), a club based in Germany, has over eight thousand members and twenty-six chapters, including one each in Canada and the United States. Breed wardens examine coat and conformation, and dogs must pass a series of field performance tests before they're allowed to pass on their genes. Puppies produced in North America are registered in Germany, and tattooed with identifying numbers in their ears before leaving the breeder's kennel.

Wirehair pups do not come cheap: $500 and up, compared to around $300 for a German shorthair of good field breeding. Buying a puppy from a registered Verein Deutsch-Drahthaar breeder (there are approximately fifty in North America) will assure a hunter of getting a prospect from tested parents. Wirehairs are also registered with the American Kennel Club (1,162 dogs in

1990), the parent organization for the German Wirehair Pointer Club of America. Some of these dogs hunt, some do not. The North American Versatile Hunting Dog Association (NAVHDA) has a widely respected testing program aimed at the continental breeds; consider high NAVHDA scores by parents when evaluating an AKC-registered litter.

Summary: Medium to large. Close to moderate working range, quicker and livelier than most continentals. Keen nose. Points and retrieves all gamebirds. Good duck retriever. Wire coat repels briars and water. Temperament generally good, but some wirehairs are dangerously aggressive. Intelligent, precocious, sometimes prankish. Deutsch drahthaar a tested field performer; AKC-registered German wirehaired pointer more variable in temperament, hunting ability, and desire.

Resources

"Drahthaar!," Buz Fawcett, *Gun Dog*, November/December 1985.

Verein Deutsch-Drahthaar Group North America: Ronald K. Mason, 11825 Lanceshire Circle, Oklahoma City, OK 73162.

German Wirehaired Pointer Club of America, Laurie McCarty, 2506 Ann Arbor Ln., Bowie, MD 20716.

Vizsla

According to one source, "vizsla" comes from a Hungarian word meaning "responsively alert." Another account says vizsla is Turkish for "to seek." A third reference identifies Vizsla as a hamlet, now vanished, in Hungary's Danube River valley.

One book maintains that the vizsla—the modern-day versatile hunting dog—stems from the canines brought by the Magyars from the Asian steppes into what is now Hungary, around the fourth century. Another version has the breed spinning off from the Weimaraner (which it resembles) in the late 1800s. Or perhaps it derives from a mix of the Turkish "yellow dog" (the Turks ruled Hungary during the sixteenth and seventeenth centuries) and a native Magyar hound . . . .

Whatever its origin, the vizsla (pronounced VEESH-la) is a distinctive breed considered the national hunting dog of Hungary. It arose in Hungary's high central plains as a pointer and retriever of partridge and quail abundant in that dry, grain-growing region.

The vizsla almost died out in the chaos following both world wars. When the Soviets occupied Hungary in 1945, many Hungarians fled to other parts of the world, some taking their dogs

The vizsla has a short, copper-colored coat and hunts in a light-footed, graceful manner.

with them. By 1960 the breed had become popular enough in the United States to warrant recognition by the American Kennel Club.

The vizsla presents a striking appearance: sleek, short-haired, athletically muscular, with a deep chest tapering back to narrow hips. The artist Robert Abbett has noted, "The vizsla's anatomy, like the pointer's, is close to the surface." But the vizsla's most distinctive feature is its color: a warm rusty gold described in Hungarian as sarga, or "breadcrust." The rusty gold coloring extends to the nose, eyes, and the inside of the mouth.

Males stand twenty-two to twenty-four inches at the withers and weigh fifty to sixty-five pounds; females are about two inches shorter and ten pounds lighter. The vizsla is lighter-boned and rangier than the German shorthaired pointer. The shorthair's tail is trimmed by two-thirds, so that only a third remains; in the vizsla the tail is docked by only about one third, giving it a somewhat racier appearance. The vizsla's sleek fur has no undercoat and requires little grooming. With its thin coat, it is better adapted to hot than to cold weather.

The vizsla hunts in a light-footed, graceful manner. In spite of its lean muscularity, it does not have the pace and range of a field-trial pointer or English setter. The vizsla is a thorough, close- to medium-range worker on grouse, woodcock, pheasant, and other upland birds, including quail in smaller coverts. Most vizslas take to the water readily and can be used for limited duck retrieving, or for fetching upland birds that have fallen on the wrong side of a creek or slough.

The typical vizsla has an outstanding nose, a strong pointing instinct, and a natural propensity to retrieve. The vizsla is one of the easiest of the versatile breeds to train, thanks to its intense desire to please: Some breed authorities assert that it likes people perhaps even a bit more than it likes to hunt. A sensitive dog, the vizsla responds best to patience, praise, and encouragement. It can be ruined by harsh treatment.

Vizslas are gentle with children and make excellent, affectionate household pets, often with a strong protective instinct. Vizsla owners almost uniformly recommend against kenneling the breed for long periods.

Show vizslas may be totally unsuitable in the field; the Vizsla Club of America can recommend breeders of hunting stock. The club sponsors a Versatility Program that tests for conformation, obedience, and field skills. A dog passing the conformation exam will have CC following its name on its pedigree; OC connotes an obedience certificate; and FD certifies some degree of skill in hunting, pointing, and retrieving. Dogs that pass all three tests will have VC after their names. Vizslas are also tested by the North American Versatile Hunting Dog Association (NAVHDA), the National Shoot to Retrieve Association (NSTRA), and other similar groups. The American Kennel Club registered 1,750 vizslas in 1990.

About sixty years ago, a new breed was created in Hungary by crossing the vizsla with the drahthaar (German wirehaired pointer). Thanks to its thick, bristly fur, the wirehaired vizsla is more at home in cold water and briars than is its thinner-coated cousin. The breed—sometimes called "the versatile uplander"—retains the vizsla's coppery color. It is recognized in Europe and Canada but not in the United States. As of 1988, there were less than thirty wirehaired vizslas in North America.

Summary: Medium-size, thin-skinned. Strong pointing, fetching instincts. Close- to medium-range worker. Hunts all upland birds; can be used for light-duty duck retrieving. Works well in hot weather. Sensitive; may be ruined by harsh training. Gentle with children, strongly protective, good watchdog.

Resources

The Vizsla, B. C. Boggs. Glen Brier Publ., Jackson, OH, 1982.
"The Vizsla," James B. Spencer. *Gun Dog*, January/February 1985.

Vizsla Club of America: Jan Bouman, 15744 Hampshire Ave S., Prior Lake, MN 55372.

The Weimaraner is comparable in size to the German shorthaired pointer, which is a better hunting prospect.

Weimaraner

M aybe it was the sleek, exotic appearance, or the origin as a dog of the German nobility, or simply the breed's rareness in this country, but for some reason the sporting press in the late 1940s became enamored of the Weimaraner (pronounced VI-mar-ahner). Here, they trumpeted, was a dog that could do it all: hunt quail when only a few months old, track mountain lions, fetch ducks from swift current, find lost children at the ends of days-old trails. For a while, it seemed, everyone had to have a super-dog, a "gray ghost," as this short-coated import came to be known. Breeders churned out puppies that fetched five hundred dollars and up—quite a price in the 1950s.

Naturally, the Weimaraner failed to live up to its advance billing. In the rush to sell dogs, breeders paid too little attention to traits like hunting ability and temperament. Hunters were disappointed in Weimaraners that could not outfetch Labradors or outpoint setters. Not only did the Weimaraner quickly slip from favor, it earned a reputation as a second-rate dog. Forty years later, it is just beginning to emerge from under this cloud.

The Weimaraner may have existed as far back as the seventeenth century; a 1631 painting shows a gray-coated dog that looks much like the Weimaraner of today. The breed first came into prominence around 1800 in the court of the Grand Duke Karl August of Weimar, a city south of Berlin. Karl and his fellow nobles used Weimaraners to trail deer, bear, boar, and wolves; and, when the big game dwindled, to point and retrieve birds. The breed is thought to stem from various hounds, with additions of pointing dog blood when the switch to feathered game was made.

Through the nineteenth century, the German upper class bred a limited number of Weimaraners under exceedingly strict— some might say secretive—guidelines. When a Weimaraner Club of Germany emerged in 1897, its goal was to protect the breed rather than to promote it. To keep only the very best animals as breeding stock, the total number of dogs allowed to be registered was limited to fifteen hundred.

A Rhode Island advertising executive named Howard Knight imported the first two Weimaraners into the United States in 1929. To do so, Knight had to join the Weimaraner Club of Germany, where he was accepted only after a struggle; then he found out the dogs he'd bought had been rendered sterile. If they could not be bred, they nevertheless made good hunters, and Knight, impressed, finally succeeded in getting three more Weimaraners, which became the foundation for the breed in North America. In 1941 the Weimaraner Club of America was founded, in 1943 the American Kennel Club gave official recognition, and about two years after World War II, the number of importations from Germany skyrocketed.

The Weimaraner is sturdy and strong-looking, comparable in size to the German shorthair. Males measure twenty-five to twenty-seven inches at the shoulder, females twenty-three to twenty-five inches. Effective weights are fifty to seventy pounds, with heavier specimens less suited to working in the field. The coat is short, flat, and dense, in various shades of gray from

Wirehaired Pointing
GRIFFON

Eduard Karel Korthals had a dream—some might call it an obsession. An avid hunter and the son of a wealthy Dutch munitions manufacturer, in the 1870s young Korthals decided he would develop a superior strain of versatile rough-coated hunting dog. His father, who considered dogs "insignificant animals" (he himself bred cattle for a hobby), refused to subsidize the venture. So Eduard, dogs in tow, left Holland and went to Germany.

He settled at the estate of Prince Albrecht of Solms, a pioneer in developing the German shorthaired pointer. Albrecht agreed to back Korthals in his quest. Korthals traveled throughout Belgium, Holland, France, and Germany, searching for foundation stock. He chose from among dogs that had long been called "griffons" (the name, it is thought, comes from the fierce mythological beast, half lion and half eagle, a common heraldic emblem). These dogs descended from hunting spaniels, pointers, and otter

Because it works close to the gun, the wirehaired pointing griffon performs well in smaller coverts.

hounds. Korthals ended up with eight, all having the temperament, hunting instincts, and coat characteristics he prized—and
from this nucleus a breed was born.

The wirehaired pointing griffon is slightly smaller than the
closely related German wirehaired pointer, and not quite as lively
or energetic in the field. Males are from twenty-one and a half to
twenty-three and a half inches at the shoulder, females about two
inches shorter. The average weight is fifty pounds. The griffon is
compact, solid, and heavily muscled, with a close-coupled build
contributing to endurance and stamina rather than speed. The
tail is docked to about six inches. Bristly brows overhang the
eyes, and the squarish muzzle sports a "moustache" of long hair.
One writer characterized the breed as "a classic shaggy dog that
looks as if it were put together with spare parts."

The coat that Korthals so carefully selected for requires more
upkeep than that of the sleeker continentals—the vizsla, Weimaraner, and German shorthaired pointer, but provides excellent
protection in any cover. Its outer layer is tough, harsh, and wiry, a
bit longer than that of the German wirehair. Beneath this covering lies an insulating layer of finer, denser fur. Along with the
wirehair, the griffon is the most cold-resistant of all the pointing
breeds. Coat color in most griffons consists of dark liver patches
on a steel- or silver-gray background, often with ticking.

European hunters use the dog on upland birds, rabbits and
hares, foxes, roe deer, and wild boar. The griffon trails big game
and points small game and retrieves it from land and water. It will
hunt all of the upland birds and has an excellent reputation as a
woodcock dog. Most griffons love the wet and gladly retrieve
from streams and lakes. The griffon has a strong pointing instinct, although its pointing style—thanks at least in part to its
shaggy coat—often appears undramatic. It handles easily, is
a deliberate, thorough worker, and, by nature, stays close to

the gun. The breed is a prime choice for the hunter who works smaller coverts, likes to move slowly, and wants a dog in constant contact.

Its temperament separates the griffon from the German wirehaired pointer (which was split off from the griffon at the close of the last century). The griffon thrives in the house and languishes in the kennel. It is more people-oriented than the wirehair, less independent, more anxious to please—a good choice for an inexperienced trainer. To get the most out of a griffon, give it lots of praise and encouragement.

After starting his program in Germany, Korthals moved to France, where he fully developed his breed: To this day the griffon is thought of as a French dog, and it is known in France as "Korthals' griffon." The griffon gained a reputation for durability, bravery, intelligence, and an exceptional desire to please its master. The German sporting writer Hegewald, a pseudonym for Baron von Sedlitz, wrote in a hunting magazine about the griffon: "The achievement of more practical colors, better noses, [and] heightened trainability is scarcely possible."

Some of the first griffons imported to North America were brought to New Jersey around 1900 by Louis Thebaud, who also helped establish the Brittany here. In the 1920s, two Montanans imported griffons; the breed caught on there, and today Montana, several other western states, and the Pacific Northwest have perhaps the highest concentration of griffons in America. The dogs are also seen in California, the East, and the Midwest.

The wirehaired pointing griffon has never been widely known in the United States; an estimated twelve hundred dogs exist here today. While the breed hasn't suffered a loss of quality from overbreeding for the pet industry, it *has* produced a number of poor-quality gun dogs. No doubt the Europeans sent over many rejects, and nonhunting American breeders have been admittedly indiscriminating. The griffon has always been prone to fungal infections of the ears; recently, more serious problems have begun cropping up, including soft fluffy coats, poor nerves (evinced by gunshyness and fear of people), hip dysplasia, and weak hunting desire.

In 1984 the Wirehaired Pointing Griffon Club of America announced a bold program to improve the breed. They began importing wirehaired hunting dogs from Czechoslovakia called fouseks, and crossbreeding them to griffons. (Interestingly, when the fousek was in trouble in the 1920s, infusions of griffon blood helped restore it.) More important, American griffon enthusiasts launched a strict, comprehensive testing program. Tests—not trials—reward individuals that fulfill a standard; these dogs are then certified for breeding. A Natural Ability Test examines young dogs, and an Intermediate Hunting Dog Test scrutinizes older griffons. The tests, cooperative rather than competitive events, resemble those used by the North American Versatile Hunting Dog Association to evaluate all the continental breeds. At present, there is a waiting list for puppies from certified griffon litters.

Summary: Medium-size, close-working, deliberate; points and retrieves all upland gamebirds, retrieves ducks from water. Resistant to cold; coat requires frequent grooming. People-oriented, affectionate, good choice for novice trainer. Quality varies widely within breed; best hunters from certified parents.

Resources

"The Wirehaired Pointing Griffon," Rick Van Etten. *Gun Dog*, July/August 1986.

"How to Improve a Breed," Larry Mueller. *Outdoor Life*, January 1988.

"A Breed in Need," Jerome B. Robinson. *Sports Afield,* October 1989.

The Gun Dog Supreme, breed magazine of the Wirehaired Pointing Griffon Club of North America: Joan Bailey, 11739 S.W. Beaverton Hwy. #201, Beaverton, OR 97005.

Other Europeans

In addition to the six continental breeds covered earlier, several other European hunting dogs are available in North America, although they are relatively scarce: It can be difficult to find a puppy. On the plus side, most of these dogs have been imported and bred as hunters, so there is little chance of inadvertently picking an individual out of pet stock that lacks the instinct to hunt.

PUDELPOINTER

As its name implies, the pudelpointer is a cross between the poodle and the pointer—the poodle for its protective coat and retrieving instinct, the pointer for its birdiness, stamina, and range. Germans developed the breed in the late 1800s (the foundation stud was the best pointer in the kennel of Kaiser Friedrich II), a period when many Europeans were experimenting with dog breeding and trying to develop versatile, all-around hunting dogs.

The pudelpointer stands twenty-three inches at the shoulder

and weighs fifty-five pounds. Its coat is solid brown (various shades from light to almost black), dense and wiry, quick-drying, not as long as the fur of the German wirehair and wirehaired pointing griffon. The pudelpointer is a highly intelligent dog. Like the other continentals, it points and retrieves upland game and fetches waterfowl.

Because of its strong pointer background (the breed is essentially three-quarters pointer, one-quarter poodle), the average pudelpointer is a faster, harder-driving hunter than most other continentals. The pudelpointer thrives on work, discipline, and living indoors with master and family.

The breed is recognized by the Field Dog Stud Book. The Pudelpointer Club of North America has its own registry, and accepts only those dogs that pass field tests demonstrating natural hunting ability and a willingness to accept training. The club exercises control over breeding by its members, and works to place puppies with masters who will hunt, train, and test their dogs to breed standards. The pudelpointer has excelled in North American Versatile Hunting Dog Association tests.

Resources

"Rare, But Proven," Dave Duffey. *Gun Dog*, March/April 1986.
Pudelpointer Club of North America: Bodo Winterhelt, 4039 West Ave. N3, Quartz Hill, CA 93551.

SMALL MUNSTERLANDER

The small Munsterlander comes from northern Germany, where it was once known as the Heidewachtel, or heathland quail dog. It is said to date back to the thirteenth century. It is a small dog, about the size of the English springer spaniel: twenty to twenty-two inches and forty to fifty pounds. The small Munsterlander points its game and retrieves with great enthusiasm and likes the water.

Facially, the small Munsterlander also somewhat resembles the springer, with a lively, alert physiognomy. The breed shows a range of colors similar to that of the German shorthaired and wirehaired pointers: white with roan or chestnut patches, brown with white zones heavily ticked with brown. The coat is wavy, with feathering on the backs of the legs and the tail, which is left undocked.

Vivacious, intelligent, biddable, and adaptable, the small Munsterlander makes a good family member and an alert watchdog. Breed warden Paul Jensen estimates there are only about a hundred on this continent (the small Munsterlander is more popular in Germany and Scandinavia). The Munsterlander Club of North America takes in both the small Munsterlander and the large Munsterlander, a separate breed.

Resources

"The Small Munsterlander Pointer," Paul Jensen. *Gun Dog*, March/April 1985.

Jaegerbakkens Kennel: Vibeke and Paul Jensen, 150 Hunters Ridge Rd., Concord, MA 01742.

LARGE MUNSTERLANDER

The large Munsterlander is a medium-size versatile gun dog, twenty-three to twenty-six inches at the shoulder and fifty to sixty-five pounds. Color is black-and-white, varying from predominantly white to predominantly black; white areas often have dark ticking. The head is black, sometimes with a white star or blaze on the forehead. The coat is similar to the English setter's: medium-length, thick, and wavy. The tail, which is not docked, has ample feathering.

According to Josef Schmutz of Saskatoon, Canada, secretary of the Munsterlander Club of North America, "The large Munsterlander has much to offer the upland/waterfowl hunter who also wants a cooperative, attractive, and intelligent family dog." The large Munsterlander has a lively, springy gait and a medium-range hunting pattern: 50 to 150 yards, depending on the cover. It points, can be used on a variety of upland birds, is a good trailer of running or wounded game, and retrieves from land and water. The large Munsterlander tends to be a one-person dog that prefers to hunt for its master. It makes a calm, affectionate house pet and a good watchdog.

Several hundred large Munsterlanders have been bred in North America since their introduction in 1966; foundation stock is periodically imported from Europe. At present, four kennels (three of them in Canada) breed large Munsterlanders. The Munsterlander Club of North America provides guidelines for breeding, and a club-appointed breed warden reviews all proposed matings. Puppies are eligible for registration with the North American Versatile Hunting Dog Association.

Resources

"The Large Munsterlander," Rick Van Etten. *Gun Dog*, November/December 1987.

Munsterlander News, Sheila Schmutz, R.R. 2, Box 123, Saskatoon, Saskatchewan, Canada S7K 3J5.

GERMAN LONGHAIRED POINTER

Probably fewer than one hundred German longhairs exist in North America, yet the breed has the potential to become more widespread. In Germany, it is the third most popular hunting dog, behind the German wirehair and German shorthair. The longhair is valued for its calm, cooperative nature, versatile hunting ability, and handsome, functional coat.

The breed descends from longhaired "hawking" dogs of medieval times—large land spaniels trained to locate gamebirds for falconers and later to point birds that were then caught in nets. Nineteenth-century breeders may have shaped the longhair with additions of the Gordon setter and flat-coated retriever.

The German longhair stands twenty-three to twenty-seven inches and weighs fifty to sixty-five pounds. It has a deep chest and a fairly heavy bone structure. The dense coat resists water, insulates against cold, and wards off briars. Color ranges from solid brown (the most common pattern) to combinations of white and brown. The solid-color German longhair somewhat resembles an Irish setter or a flat-coated retriever. A close- to medium-range worker, the longhair will hunt and point all the upland birds and retrieve ducks from water. In Europe, it is also used to trail and flush out big game, including deer and wild boar.

The German longhair is recognized as a breed by the Canadian Kennel Club and the North American Versatile Hunting Dog Association. At present, German breeders are interested in establishing a nucleus of North American breeders to help preserve and enlarge the longhair's gene pool. Del Peterson, a Washingtonian who has had longhairs for almost twenty years, advocates a testing and evaluation program similar to the one used in Europe to maintain excellence in conformation, temperament, and hunting ability. Peterson will serve as an intermediary for those with a sincere desire to own and hunt with a German longhair.

Resources

"The German Longhair," Rick Van Etten. *Gun Dog*, October/ November 1989.

German Longhaired Pointer Club of America: Del Peterson, 11 McKee Rd., Selah, WA 98942.

SPINONE

The spinone (pronounced spee-NO-nay) is a versatile wire-haired pointing dog from Italy. Apparently an old (perhaps even an ancient) type, it is claimed by some to be the ancestor of several other European wire-haired breeds.

A large, powerful dog, the spinone stands twenty-three to twenty-eight inches and weighs sixty to eighty pounds. The outer coat is thick, dry, and stiff, one and a half to two and a half inches long; the undercoat is downy. Colors are solid white, white patched or spotted with orange, or white and brown roan. The wiry hair forms eyebrows and a beard.

Like most of the continentals, spinones are cooperative and attuned to their masters. They are said to be good-natured, sometimes with a clownish streak. In the field they work close to the gunner and are suitable for hunting small parcels of cover at a leisurely pace. They have an intriguing pointing style: When closing in on scent, they move cautiously and may even creep like a cat. They are strong swimmers and natural retrievers.

The breed is eligible for registry in the Field Dog Stud Book and with the North American Versatile Hunting Dog Association. According to the Spinone Club of America, there are over three hundred spinones in North America today.

Resources

"The Italian Spinone," Rick Van Etten. *Gun Dog*, January/ February 1989.

The Spinone Club of America: Jim Channon, P.O. Box 258, Warsaw, VA 22572.

IV

CHOOSING A BREED

*The grouse dog is far and
away the most important ad-
junct to the sport. . . . Grouse
hunting without a dog is not
grouse hunting at all.*

—WILLIAM HARNDEN FOSTER
New England Grouse Shooting

The key to choosing the right breed of hunting dog lies in asking yourself pertinent questions about your needs, likes, dislikes, and abilities, and honestly answering them.

Do you want a dog strictly to retrieve waterfowl? If so, your task is relatively simple: You have seven breeds to choose from.

If you are not a waterfowl specialist, you will be picking from around thirty breeds. While that sounds like quite a number, one question should cut it in half: Do you want a dog that points game or flushes it?

Some things to consider:

In dense cover, a pointing dog will give you fewer actual shots on game than a flushing dog, but the shots will tend to be better

ones: Having more advance warning, you will connect on a greater percentage of birds that have been pointed. In more open
cover, a pointing dog will explore more territory than a flushing
dog and ultimately may find more birds.

A pointing dog will require a higher level of training, but if only
half-trained it will "bump" birds, flush them unexpectedly, usually
beyond shotgun range. A half-trained flushing dog, as long as it
works close to you (which, by its nature, it should want to do),
will still produce shootable birds.

Training a pointing dog calls for fields and birds and time—
lots of time. Many of a flushing dog's lessons can be given quickly
(and inexpensively) using retrieving dummies in the yard.

Most flushing dogs—spaniels, and retrievers trained to hunt
like spaniels—fetch naturally. While some pointing dogs do a good
job of retrieving, many do not. Generally speaking, a spaniel or a
retriever will recover more cripples than a pointing dog. How important is it that your dog find and bring back birds you have shot?

Perhaps the biggest question is one of aesthetics. Which strikes
your eye as more beautiful, a dog gliding through the cover and
abruptly halting on point—or a dog charging in to drive a bird
into the air, then fetching it once it is downed?

Assuming you have determined which category of dog (retrieving, flushing, or pointing) is for you, the next question is: What
kind of birds do you hunt?

Are you a dyed-in-the-wool grouse and woodcock hunter who
rarely tries for other game? Do you hunt desert quail in the oak
scrub and cholla? Do you hike the windswept shortgrass uplands
for sharp-tailed grouse and prairie chickens? Do you hunt from a
river's-edge blind, calling in Canada geese as well as ducks? Do
bobwhite quail excite you like no other bird? Is your hunting
limited to pheasants at a preserve?

A specialist will find it easier to choose a breed than will a
generalist. For each type of gamebird, there are a handful of dogs
that do excellent work.

I, like the majority of hunters, am anything but a specialist. I hunt pheasants in weed patches, ducks in marshes, woodcock in alder tangles, grouse in thornapples, and doves in cornfields. My struggle to pick a breed—to know myself as a hunter—may help other generalists make their choices.

Six years ago, when I decided to get a hunting dog, I made a list of all the kinds of hunting I do, and one other kind (jump-shooting for ducks) that I hoped to do. Then I read every article and book I could find about dogs. Books on training. Articles on little-known breeds. Chapters dealing with dogs in books about grouse hunting, pheasant hunting, duck hunting. I talked to owners of gun dogs, asked questions, and generally found these hunters biased but useful sources of information. I attended field trials. I angled for, and received, invitations to hunt behind various breeds.

I decided I lacked the patience, and did not want to spend the time acquiring the skill, to train a pointing dog up to a proper level of field performance. In the thick places where I hunt, I preferred knowing at all times where the dog was. And I very much wanted a dog to fetch what I shot.

A small dog, since I live in a small house. A friendly dog, but one that would let me know when a car came down the lane. One whose coat wouldn't require an ungodly amount of grooming. A dog whose color, carriage, and way of working pleased my eye.

According to my various sources, the English springer spaniel filled the bill. Small enough to live in close quarters, it had a pleasant disposition and was easy to train; it hunted close to the gun; it loved to fetch; it was small enough to live in close quarters; it retrieved from the water in any but the coldest weather; it could handle just about any winged game smaller than a Canada goose; and, an added bonus, it was widely available in good hunting bloodlines. And when I looked at photographs, I saw a sturdy, rough-and-ready dog that looked good even when slathered with mud.

I am happy to report that the English springer turned out to be just the breed for me. It's not the right dog for every hunter. A springer doesn't point, of course. It would be a ludicrous choice for certain kinds of game in certain types of cover—for quail in big fields, or scaup in cold coastal waters. And no doubt springers look anything but handsome to some people. But for my personality and circumstances, and the hunting conditions and gamebirds of central Pennsylvania, a springer was the right choice.

If you've read the general chapters on the three hunting dog categories, you should have an understanding of how each type works in the field. Now let's zero in on the gamebirds, and discuss the dogs—including specific breeds—that can be expected to handle them.

Pheasant

The ring-necked pheasant, a native of Asia, has been introduced and naturalized over much of northern North America. It is the primary gamebird offered by shooting preserves.

If you want to hunt with a pointing dog, consider one of the continentals, especially the Brittany, German shorthair, and German wirehair (all used extensively as shooting dogs on commercial preserves). Most of the European dogs work pheasants quite adequately, pointing, trailing cripples, and fetching. In open country, such as in the Plains states, a wider-ranging dog will make more finds: an English setter, pointer, or red setter.

Because pheasants like to run, a flushing dog will produce more birds than will a pointer. The top pheasant dog is the English springer spaniel, which covers the ground a bit more thoroughly and exuberantly than the Labrador and the golden retrievers, which also are excellent. The American water, Boykin, and English cocker spaniels can give good service, as can the Chesapeake Bay retriever and the other less-well-known retriever breeds. An advantage to hunting pheasants with flushing spaniels and retrievers is that these dogs are natural, soft-mouthed retrievers.

RUFFED GROUSE

Ruffed grouse do not run as consistently or as far as ring-necked pheasants, but they do run, especially where hunted heavily. For most hunters, a close-working flushing spaniel is the best bet: It will show the hunter more shootable birds, and retrieve them. The English springer, English cocker, and Boykin spaniel are excellent, while the slightly slower American water spaniel may be just the ticket for the person who likes a more leisurely hunt. Welsh, Clumber, Sussex, and field spaniels, which have been heavily influenced by show breeding, offer much less potential. Among the retrievers, the golden, Labrador, Nova Scotia duck tolling, and flat-coated retrievers do well on grouse.

The grouse purist will probably insist on a pointing dog. The best of these cover a great deal of terrain and locate and pin down their quarry with a fast, unerring approach. Owners of these canine athletes devote hundreds of their own hours—or pay professional trainers—to develop and maintain their dogs. English setters and pointers can be superb grouse dogs; the setter, with its thicker coat, has a slight edge in colder country. The Brittany handles easily and tends to work at a closer range than the setter and pointer; it is a good choice for the beginning trainer. As a grouse performer it is followed by the German short-haired pointer, German wirehaired pointer, and the other continentals.

Woodcock

The woodcock breeds from Nova Scotia west to Manitoba, then migrates to wintering grounds in Louisiana and Mississippi. It is hunted mainly in the northern part of its range. The woodcock holds well for pointing dogs, which often find it in the same coverts as ruffed grouse. Any of the pointing dogs will work woodcock, although some will not care to retrieve these smallish, strong-smelling birds.

All spaniels love to flush woodcock, and most will also fetch them. The cocker, or "'cocking," spaniel was named for its particular suitability for hunting the European woodcock: The field-bred English cocker is an excellent, traditional choice. Retrievers will work woodcock, but many are less willing than spaniels to dive into the rampant cover where these birds are usually found.

Bobwhite Quail

The bobwhite is found throughout the southeastern United States, west to Texas and north to South Dakota and New York. Pointing dogs are the premier quail hunters, ranging widely to locate scattered coveys. Quail generally hold well for any of the pointing breeds.

The pointer has long been the top choice for bobwhite, especially where the weather is warm. The English setter is also an excellent quail dog. Where cover is broken up into smaller parcels, the continental breeds do well, especially the Brittany and German shorthair. And when quail resort to thickets—during winter in the northern part of their range, or when hunted heavily —one of the flushing or retrieving breeds can roust them out.

SHARP-TAILED GROUSE, PRAIRIE CHICKEN, SAGE GROUSE, HUNGARIAN PARTRIDGE

Breeds that excel on bobwhite quail also do well on these four midwestern and western game birds: Top choices are pointers, English setters, and the bigger-going strains of German shorthairs and Brittanys. Young sharp-tailed grouse and prairie chickens hold well for pointing dogs, but as the birds mature they grow warier, running and often flushing wild. Many gunners rely on close-working flushing spaniels and retrievers, especially the English springer and the Labrador retriever.

DESERT QUAIL AND CHUKAR PARTRIDGE

Harlequin, scaled, California, Gambel's, and mountain quail are native to the desert Southwest, California, and parts of the Northwest; the chukar has been introduced widely in the West. Most of these birds would rather run than fly. The harlequin is an exception, usually holding tightly when confronted by a dog. Among the pointing dogs, English setters, Brittanys, German shorthairs, and pointers are logical choices, with the closer-coated breeds getting the nod in hot weather. The Labrador retriever and English springer spaniel make excellent desert quail dogs, breaking up coveys and fetching downed birds.

Dᴏᴠᴇs

A dove hunter needs a good retriever that can be taught to sit still and fetch on command. Boykin and English springer spaniels work nicely as nonslip retrievers and in jump-shooting for doves along crop-field edges. Since doves are usually hunted in warm weather, the short-haired Labrador retriever is also a logical pick. The continental pointing breeds will fetch doves, with the German shorthair and vizsla top performers. One of the English pointing breeds would be a poor choice for doves.

Wᴀᴛᴇʀғᴏwʟ

The dedicated waterfowler needs a solid retrieving dog. The Labrador and Chesapeake Bay retrievers have proven themselves over the years. When the game is geese and the water is icy, go with a big, tough-minded Chesapeake, also the breed of choice for bay and sea ducks such as redhead, scaup, goldeneye, and eider. A waterfowler who frequently hunts the uplands will be nicely served by a golden, Labrador, flat-coated, or Nova Scotia duck tolling retriever.

Many hunters go for ducks only occasionally, or take them incidentally when hunting other game. For early-season inland water work, an English springer, Boykin, or American water spaniel will do nicely. The continental breeds, encouraged and properly trained, will also fetch ducks: German wirehair, pudel-pointer, wirehaired pointing griffon, and German shorthair, among others.

Blue Grouse, Spruce Grouse, Ptarmigan

These northern gallinaceous birds (and also the ruffed grouse) can be quite tame where they are little hunted. The flushing breeds, spaniels and retrievers, offer the best sport and will round up cripples. It is not conducive to a pointing dog's steadiness to have a big enticing bird like a ptarmigan walk up to the dog on point, stand there, and croak at it.

Eight breeds have emerged as the top American bird dogs of our era, widely available in solid hunting bloodlines. By doing a little homework, asking around, watching dogs of several strains in action—and by honestly evaluating your own training abilities and hunting preferences—you stand an excellent chance of getting a fine hunter from any of these breeds.

Flushing spaniels: English springer.

Retrievers: Labrador, Chesapeake Bay, golden.

Pointing dogs: English setter, pointer, German shorthaired pointer, Brittany.

If, on the other hand, one of the less-popular breeds catches your eye or fires your imagination, don't hesitate to go after it. Be prepared to work harder, do more research, follow up on leads, perhaps wait a year or longer—and finally, order a dog from halfway across the continent if you must. It is through such quests that the more obscure breeds survive and continue to offer hunters a delightful wealth of dogs.

V

PICKING A PUPPY

*The size of the puppy and its
vulnerability bring something
out in the handler. . . . You
coax and compliment and
overlook mistakes. You find
training sessions fun and the
pup's enthusiasm infectious.*

—GEOFFREY NORMAN
The Orvis Book of Upland Bird Shooting

An acquaintance recently told me how he got his German wire-haired pointer. It seems the dog had been running wild in, of all places, downtown Boston. People had pitied it and fed it; finally, with winter coming, someone took it to a veterinarian and got shots for it, then found a breeder who agreed to adopt the dog. My friend, in scouting around for a wirehair, heard about this waif, went and looked at it, and bought it. Since it didn't come with papers, he doesn't know the dog's age or its breeding. But it has turned out to be a pretty decent hunter. It points, works at a reasonable pace and range, and fetches. My friend likes the dog, and it likes him.

That's an odd way to pick a bird dog, but at least my friend could look the animal over before paying for it, and see that it had potential. Far worse is to walk into a pet store and plunk down cash for an unknown quantity panting and grinning behind bars. Dogs bred for the store market usually come from puppy mills, where sires and dams are indiscriminately matched to churn out warm, cuddly puppies—canines whose likelihood of becoming hunters, even if from traditional hunting breeds, are slim to nonexistent. Almost as risky is to buy through a newspaper classified ad: These are mostly show- and pet-stock dogs whose owners thought it would be fun to have a litter of puppies. Their fun will become your folly should you decide to buy.

In the course of picking a breed, learn all that you can about your choice. Read articles in hunting magazines, especially *Gun Dog*, a bimonthly that runs a detailed feature on a different breed each issue. (Check back issues in a library, or find a local subscriber.) If your prospective breed has a national interest club, join it. Study the club newsletter. Attend field trials and hunting tests; wangle hunts with several representatives of the breed. Talk with owners of dogs that hunt and handle in a way you would feel comfortable with. If you see a champion or a hunter you like, try to get a pup from it, or from its dam or sire.

Consult a professional hunting dog trainer in your area. Most specialize in one or a few breeds; if the trainer doesn't concentrate on your breed, he or she will probably know someone who does, and that person will be glad to help you, since you may ultimately buy a dog or pay for its training.

If the trainer is not a commercial breeder, he or she will put you in touch with one. Try to find a litter in your own area. This is much simpler than having a puppy shipped from a distant state, and presumably you will be selecting from a strain bred to hunt your local gamebirds. (It would be a chancy business to order up a pointer, say, from the Oklahoma quail country to use on grouse in upstate New York.) The classified ads of sporting magazines, especially *Gun Dog*, are a good source for breeders of hunting dogs.

Don't rule out hobby breeders, hunters and field trialers who often produce healthy, well-socialized puppies of excellent breeding. When looking at a litter, check on the sire and dam. Ask to see them worked on game, although this may be hard to arrange: The dam may not be able to, since she has just delivered puppies and may still be nursing them; and in many cases the breeder will not own the sire, having sent his bitch away to be serviced by an excellent dog. If possible, take along someone who knows the breed. Ask the breeder for names of hunters who have shot over one or both of the parents. If you're shopping from a commercial breeder, get a list of people who have bought puppies in the past. Don't be lazy: Thoroughly checking these references may save you heartache later on.

Learn to interpret pedigrees. Dogs registered by the Field Dog Stud Book are almost always field trial or hunting types; in this registry, "Ch." stands for field champion. In the papers of dogs registered with the American Kennel Club, "CH," means "show champion." In some AKC breeds—the flat-coated retriever, for instance—there is no split between show and field types, and dogs may hold titles in both areas. In other breeds that formerly were widely hunted—Clumber, field, and Sussex spaniels—the pool of available dogs is now limited to show lines. In still other breeds, such as the English springer spaniel, show and field lines have totally split. If an AKC pedigree is peppered with "FC" (field trial champion), and "AFC" (amateur field trial champion), you're in business. If there are no letters preceding parents', grandparents', or great-grandparents' names, proceed carefully. Most hunting stock will have field trial champions a generation or so back.

As an index of field ability, the AKC hunting tests must be taken with a grain of salt. Many pet and show dogs have earned Junior Hunter certificates. Senior Hunter is a much stronger indicator of utility, and Master Hunter denotes an exceptional field performer. In the end, however, there is no substitute for actually watching the litter's parents in action.

Rack up a huge telephone bill, travel a thousand miles if you must, but find a breeder who produces dogs geared toward *your* type of hunting. Remember, the dog may be your hunting companion for the next ten years. If you order a pup sight unseen, deal with a reputable kennel and try to describe precisely the type of hunting you do and the kind of dog you want.

A PUPPY OR A TRAINED DOG?

Twenty years ago, buying a trained adult dog was probably more popular than it is today, when most hunters start off with puppies. There are several good reasons for investing in a trained dog: You doubt your ability to develop a hunting dog, you lack access to training grounds, you don't want to wait a year or two for a puppy to mature, you can see exactly what you're getting.

Obviously, a trained dog will cost more than a puppy. Someone

—a preserve operator, kennel owner, field trialer, breeder, or hunter whose company just transferred him or her to Saudi Arabia—put many hours into developing the dog, and deserves recompense. If you decide to buy a trained dog, be sure to see it handled by the seller, both to be certain of its ability and to learn the commands the dog has been taught.

"Started" dogs cost less than fully trained dogs. Often a started dog is sold because it does not have the drive or skills of a top-flight field-trial performer—something the original owner could not know until the dog began demonstrating its potential at six to eighteen months of age. A field-trial reject can be a terrific bargain, doing everything in the coverts that the most ardent hunter could desire.

Buying a trained or started dog has its dangers, however. You may be buying a cull. You inherit any mistakes the previous owner made. The dog may not bond to you as completely as a puppy would. You have no idea how the dog was raised: Was it properly socialized, or kept languishing in a kennel? Was it left with its littermates too long? (Animal behaviorists believe that when a litter is kept together past seven weeks, a pecking order is established, with a lower-ranking individual developing a poor opinion of itself that sticks with the dog for life, making it much harder to train.) Probably the most hopeless prospect is the adult dog that has never had any training.

To get the most out of the experience, pick a puppy. Training it will be fun, an education for you as well as the dog. Many excellent books explain how to train the various breeds. If you have a backyard and fifteen minutes of free time a day, you can do a lot toward training a dog. For more advanced lessons you'll need access to hunting cover and live birds such as pigeons, pheasants, or quail. Many areas have active bird dog clubs offering training grounds, birds, equipment, advice, and hands-on help. You can do your own basic training, then place your dog with a professional for a month or two of polishing.

You reach the pinnacle of upland hunting when you take birds over a dog you have trained yourself.

PICKING A PUPPY

There is nothing quite like going to pick a puppy: The world is a place of clarity, promise, joy—heightened by a dash of apprehension.

Your goal should be a healthy puppy, a spunky but trainable dog. Some hunters favor females, while others lean toward males. In the field, there is little difference between the sexes. Choose a dog of the gender toward which you feel more affinity.

Selecting a dog at the tender age of eight weeks is very much a crap shoot. But assuming you've found a well-bred litter, here's one way to go about picking a pup.

Spend as much time as you can with the litter, playing with the pups and observing them. If you notice a timid individual, one that consistently hangs back and seems frightened of new situations, do not consider it: To become a good gun dog, it will probably need more care and coaxing than you'll want to give it. If a pup is extra aggressive, scrapping with its littermates, shouldering them aside at the food dish, growling and maybe even nipping when you try to hold it down with your hand, leave it for some field-trialer: This pup will be a bold dog with great desire and spirit, but a real handful to train.

Concentrate on the two, three, or four "average" pups that are left. One at a time, take them out of the pen for a few simple tests. Carry the pup around, talking to it in a gentle voice. Does it enjoy the attention, or does it struggle to get down? Place the pup on the ground, run off, and call to it. Does it come to you, or wander off in another direction? Toss a pheasant wing. Does the pup ignore the wing, sniff it and walk away, or pick it up? (Pups that pick up and carry objects demonstrate a strong natural instinct to retrieve.) Which pups appear sensible, human-oriented, confident? Which seem to really like you? Finally, and most important, which one do you like best?

Keep in mind that the breeder may be able to help you choose the sort of pup you want. After all, he or she has seen the dogs interacting for almost two months.

Other factors to consider:

Some breeders claim a link between physical characteristics and behavioral traits. Let's say you find yourself in the enviable position of picking from a litter sired or borne by a top-notch bird dog. You then select the puppy whose markings most resemble those of the parent you admire, figuring that a large component of field ability and mental makeup accompany the genes that code for appearance.

The best months to buy a pup are April, May, and June. Summer is prime training time, and, if you do your part, your pup may be ready for some in-the-field practice by the time hunting season rolls around.

If you've found your prospect far from home, rest assured that puppies are routinely and safely shipped by air transport. The seller makes the arrangements and tells the buyer when to expect the crated dog; the buyer pays the shipping charge. Reputable breeders guarantee the health of their dogs. Even if you order sight unseen, the odds are good that a pup out of decent field breeding will, with proper training, develop into a satisfactory hunting dog.

REGISTER YOUR DOG

If you have any intention of ever breeding your dog, be sure to register it. You wouldn't take a chance on buying an unregistered puppy, so don't expect to be able to sell one, either. Be sure to get registry information from the breeder from whom you purchase. Or, contact the American Kennel Club, Field Dog Stud Book, or other pertinent organization.

SHOULD YOU OWN A DOG?

After rubbing elbows with enough hunters in the field and on shooting preserves, I have realized that, quite simply, a substantial percentage of them should not own bird dogs.

You should not own a dog unless you will go to the trouble of finding one with a reasonable chance of turning into the hunting partner you hope it will be. An astounding number of people buy dogs from show stock and then expect them to hunt. They waste considerable time and money, and end up miserable: Their dog still won't hunt, but they can't get rid of it because they, their spouse, or their children have become attached to the animal. A responsible hunter will learn what a given breed can be expected to do, and then find a prospect with actual field potential—a dog whose parents are both good field-trial or hunting dogs.

To get a good performance out of a dog, give it plenty of love and attention so it will want to please you. Most of the hunting breeds make good pets, and it is a fine idea to let your dog live in the house, where you will interact with it frequently. You should not own a dog if, after buying the animal, you will simply kennel it and ignore it except for giving it food and water and an occasional romp. Not only will you deprive the animal, you will deny yourself the fascinating interchange that can flow between two species of hunters wedded over thousands of years.

*Well he repays you, by a life-
time of fidelity, all the care
which you may bestow upon
him. Whatever class of dogs he
may belong to, according to
his capacity, he will studiously contribute to your
interests or your sports.*

—John Krider
Krider's Sporting Anecdotes

Appendix

The American Kennel Club: 51 Madison Ave., New York, NY 10010 (hunt tests and breed club information).

Field Dog Stud Book: American Field Publications, 542 S. Dearborn St., Chicago, IL 60605.

National Shoot to Retrieve Association: 226 N. Mill St. #2, Plainfield, IN 46168 (hunting competitions for pointing breeds).

North American Versatile Hunting Dog Association: 1700 N. Skyline Dr., Burnsville, MN 55337 (registration, training, and certification of versatile breeds).

Orthopedic Foundation for Animals: 2300 Nifong Blvd., Columbia, MO 65201 (publications on, and testing for, canine hip dysplasia).